AI FOR BEGINNERS: A SIMPLE GUIDE TO GROWING YOUR WEBSITE AND BUSINESS

FOREWORD

In the ever-evolving landscape of modern business, the integration of Artificial Intelligence (AI) is not just an option—it's an imperative. AI has transcended its status as a cutting-edge technology used only by tech giants, becoming an accessible and essential tool for businesses of all sizes. From optimizing operations to enhancing customer experiences, AI is now the driving force behind some of the most significant advancements in how we conduct business. This book is a practical guide for anyone looking to harness that power to transform their business.

As someone who has witnessed the incredible impact of AI firsthand, I've seen how it can revolutionize businesses—whether you're an online retailer looking to personalize product recommendations, a service provider wanting to automate customer support, or a content creator aiming to deliver more relevant, engaging material to your audience. The potential applications of AI are vast, and they're growing by the day.

What makes AI so powerful is its ability to turn data into actionable insights, automate repetitive tasks, and deliver personalized experiences at scale. But what sets businesses apart in the AI-driven world is not just access to the technology—it's understanding how to implement it effectively. That's where this book comes in.

This is not just another technical manual or a theoretical exploration of AI. It's a step-by-step guide filled with actionable advice on how to define your AI goals, select the right tools, and implement strategies that align with your business objectives. Whether you're a small business owner new to AI or an experienced professional looking to deepen your understanding, this book provides the roadmap you need to integrate AI into your daily operations and see real results.

The chapters ahead will walk you through the practicalities of using AI to increase website traffic, boost conversions, improve customer retention, and streamline your workflow. You'll find real-world case studies that illustrate how businesses just like yours have successfully implemented AI—and how you can do the same. You'll also learn how to overcome common challenges, from managing costs to ensuring data privacy and security, with clear, accessible solutions.

By the end of this book, you'll not only have the knowledge to implement AI in your business but the confidence to leverage its full potential. The digital age is transforming rapidly, and businesses that can adapt to these changes—using AI to their advantage—will thrive in the years to come.

It's time to embrace the future of business. AI is no longer just for the tech-savvy—it's for every business owner, entrepreneur, and professional ready to take the next step toward growth and innovation. The journey ahead is exciting, and this book is your guide.

So, turn the page and get ready to transform your business with AI.

Thanks to ChatGPT 4.0 for helping me write this book. Your guidance, creativity, and expertise have been invaluable in shaping each chapter. From brainstorming ideas to refining the final draft, your support has made this journey smoother and more enjoyable. I couldn't have done it without your consistent assistance and inspiration.

A. Wierenga

CONTENTS

Foreword
CHAPTER 1: Introduction to AI and Its Role in Websites
1.1 What is AI?

Introduction
What is AI?
Types of AI
How AI Works
Applications of AI in Websites
Why AI is Valuable for Website Owners
Conclusion: AI for Beginners
Key Takeaways
1.2 The Benefits of Using AI on Websites
Introduction
Why AI is Important for Websites
Time Savings Through Automation
   Personalization for a Better User Experience
   Data-Driven Insights and Better Decision-Making
   Improved Marketing Efficiency
   Enhanced Customer Service with AI Chatbots
   Increased Sales Through Personalization and Upselling
   Better Customer Retention and Loyalty Programs
Conclusion: AI's Impact on Website Success
Key Takeaways
1.3 AI Tools for Website Owners
Introduction

AI Tools for SEO (Search Engine Optimization)
    Surfer SEO
    Clearscope
    SEMrush

AI Tools for Content Generation and Optimization
    Jasper (formerly Jarvis)
    Copy.ai
    Frase

AI Tools for Customer Service and Engagement
    Tidio
    Drift
    LivePerson

AI Tools for Personalization
    Dynamic Yield
    Nosto
    Clerk.io

AI Tools for Marketing and Advertising
    Adext AI
    WordStream
    Revealbot

AI Tools for Email Marketing Automation
    Klaviyo
    Mailchimp
    Omnisend

Conclusion: Choosing the Right AI Tools for Your Website

CHAPTER 2: AI for Improving Website Traffic

2.1 Using AI for SEO Optimization

Introduction

What is SEO Optimization?

How AI Helps with SEO Optimization
  AI-Powered Keyword Research
    Tools for AI-Powered Keyword Research

2. AI-Driven Content Optimization

Tools for AI Content Optimization
3. AI for Competitor Analysis
   Tools for AI Competitor Analysis
4. AI for Technical SEO Audits
   Tools for AI-Driven Technical SEO Audits
5. AI for Link Building and Outreach
   Tools for AI-Driven Link Building
   How AI Helps:
6. AI for Voice Search Optimization
   Tools for Voice Search Optimization
2.2 Content Generation with AI
Introduction
What is AI-Powered Content Generation?
How AI Improves Content Creation
AI Tools for Content Generation
  Jasper (formerly Jarvis)
  Copy.ai
  Writesonic
2. Creating Blog Posts with AI
   Step-by-Step Guide to Creating a Blog Post with AI
3. Creating Product Descriptions with AI
   How AI Helps with Product Descriptions
   Social Media and Marketing Content with AI
   How AI Helps with Social Media Content
   Email Campaigns with AI
   How AI Helps with Email Marketing
Conclusion: AI as a Powerful Tool for Content Generation
Key Takeaways:
2.3 Social Media Marketing with AI
Introduction
What is AI-Powered Social Media Marketing?
How AI Enhances Social Media Marketing
   AI for Social Media Content Creation

      Tools for AI Content Creation
   AI for Social Media Scheduling and Automation
      Tools for AI-Powered Scheduling and Automation
3. AI for Audience Targeting and Personalization
      Tools for AI-Powered Audience Targeting
4. AI for Social Media Performance Analysis
      Tools for AI-Powered Performance Analysis
5. AI for Social Listening and Monitoring
      Tools for AI-Powered Social Listening
Conclusion: AI as a Game-Changer for Social Media Marketing
Key Takeaways:
CHAPTER 3: AI for Increasing Conversions and Sales
3.1 Personalization Using AI
Introduction
What is Personalization Using AI?
Why Personalization is Important
How AI Powers Personalization
Personalized Product Recommendations
     Tools for AI-Powered Product Recommendations
Personalized Content and Messaging
     Tools for AI-Powered Content Personalization
3. Personalized Email Marketing
     Tools for AI-Powered Email Personalization
4. Personalized Website Experience
     Tools for AI-Powered Website Personalization
5. Personalization for Retargeting and Remarketing
     Tools for AI-Powered Retargeting
Conclusion: The Power of AI in Personalization
Key Takeaways:
3.2 AI-Powered Email Marketing
Introduction
What is AI-Powered Email Marketing?
Why AI-Powered Email Marketing Matters

Key Benefits of AI in Email Marketing
Personalizing Email Content with AI
    Tools for AI-Powered Email Personalization
2. AI for Automated Email Campaigns
    Tools for AI-Powered Email Automation
3. AI for Audience Segmentation
    Tools for AI-Powered Audience Segmentation
4. AI for Optimizing Send Times
    Tools for AI-Powered Send Time Optimization
5. AI for Subject Line Optimization
    Tools for AI-Powered Subject Line Optimization
Conclusion: The Power of AI in Email Marketing
Key Takeaways
3.3 Chatbots and Conversational AI for Sales
Introduction
What are Chatbots and Conversational AI?
Why Use Chatbots for Sales?
How Chatbots and Conversational AI Boost Sales
  Providing Instant Customer Support
    Tools for AI-Powered Customer Support
2. Offering Personalized Product Recommendations
    Tools for Personalized Product Recommendations
3. Reducing Cart Abandonment
    Tools for Reducing Cart Abandonment
4. Collecting Customer Feedback
    Tools for AI-Powered Customer Feedback Collection
5. Supporting Customers Across Multiple Channels
    Tools for Omnichannel Chatbot Support
Conclusion: Boosting Sales with Chatbots and Conversational AI
Key Takeaways:
CHAPTER 4: AI for Managing and Scaling Your Website
4.1 Predictive Analytics and Insights
Introduction

What is Predictive Analytics?
How Predictive Analytics Works
Benefits of Predictive Analytics for Website Owners
  Predicting Customer Behavior
    Tools for Predicting Customer Behavior
  Sales Forecasting and Demand Planning
    Tools for Sales Forecasting and Demand Planning
  Optimizing Marketing Campaigns
    Tools for Predictive Marketing Insights
  Enhancing Customer Retention
    Tools for Predicting Customer Retention
  Pricing Optimization
    Tools for Pricing Optimization
Conclusion: Leveraging Predictive Analytics for Business Growth
Key Takeaways:
4.2 AI for Dynamic Pricing and Promotions
Introduction
What is Dynamic Pricing?
What are AI-Powered Promotions?
How AI Improves Dynamic Pricing and Promotions
  Dynamic Pricing with AI
    Tools for AI-Powered Dynamic Pricing
  AI-Powered Promotions and Discounts
    Tools for AI-Powered Promotions
  Optimizing Inventory and Demand with Dynamic Pricing
    Tools for Inventory and Demand Optimization
  Personalized Pricing for Different Customer Segments
    Tools for Personalized Pricing
  Competitor Monitoring and Price Matching
    Tools for Competitor Monitoring and Price Matching
  Testing and Analyzing Pricing Strategies
    Tools for Testing Pricing Strategies
Conclusion: Using AI for Dynamic Pricing and Promotions

Key Takeaways:
4.3 AI for Customer Retention
Introduction
What is Customer Retention?
Why Use AI for Customer Retention?
  Predicting Customer Churn with AI
    Tools for Predicting Customer Churn
  Personalized Re-Engagement Campaigns
    Tools for AI-Powered Re-Engagement
  Loyalty Programs Powered by AI
    Tools for AI-Driven Loyalty Programs
  Customer Feedback and Sentiment Analysis
    Tools for AI-Powered Sentiment Analysis
  Automating Retention Efforts with AI
    Tools for AI-Powered Retention Automation
  Improving the Customer Experience with AI
    Tools for Enhancing the Customer Experience
Conclusion: AI as a Tool for Retaining Customers
Key Takeaways:
CHAPTER 5: Practical Implementation and Case Studies
5.1 Step-by-Step Guide to AI Integration
Introduction
Why Integrate AI into Your Website or Business?
  Define Your AI Objectives and Use Cases
  Choose the Right AI Tools
  Collect and Organize Your Data
  Integrate AI with Your Existing Systems
  Test and Monitor Performance
  Optimize and Scale Your AI Use
Conclusion: Successfully Integrating AI into Your Business
5.2 Real-World Case Studies of AI Integration
Introduction
Case Study 1: Netflix – Personalization with AI

Case Study 2: Sephora – AI-Powered Virtual Assistant

Case Study 3: Amazon – AI for Dynamic Pricing and Inventory Management

Case Study 4: Starbucks – AI for Customer Retention and Personalization

Case Study 5: H&M – AI for Supply Chain Optimization

Conclusion: Real-World AI Successes

Key Takeaways:

5.3 Common Challenges and Solutions

Introduction

  Overcoming AI Adoption Barriers: Addressing Common Fears and Misconceptions

    Common Fears and Misconceptions About AI:

  Solutions to Overcome AI Adoption Barriers

    AI as a Job Enhancer, Not a Job Replacer

    Start Simple: User-Friendly AI Solutions

    Hybrid Decision-Making: Combining AI with Human Judgment

    Begin with High-Impact, Low-Risk AI Use Cases

  Managing Costs and ROI: How to Implement AI Affordably and Measure the Return on Investment

  How to Implement AI Affordably

    Start Small and Scale Gradually

    Leverage Cloud-Based AI Services

    Choose AI Tools with Flexible Pricing Plans

    Automate Repetitive Tasks to Maximize ROI

  How to Measure AI's Return on Investment (ROI)

    Define Clear Goals and Metrics

    Calculate Cost Savings from Automation

    Track Revenue Growth and Conversion Rates

    Analyze Long-Term Customer Retention and Satisfaction

Conclusion: Overcoming AI Adoption Barriers and Measuring ROI

Key Takeaways:

CHAPTER 6: Final Project

  6.1 Setting Up Your AI Strategy

- Introduction
- Define Your Goals: What Do You Want to Achieve with AI?
  - Common AI-Driven Goals:
- Select and Integrate AI Tools Based on Your Objectives
  - AI Tools for Common Objectives:
- Create a 3-Month AI Action Plan
  - Step 1: Month 1 - Set Up and Initial Integration
  - Step 2: Month 2 - Monitor Performance and Optimize
  - Step 3: Month 3 - Scale and Expand AI Use

Conclusion: Building a Successful AI Strategy

Key Takeaways

Conclusion: Harnessing AI for Business Growth

Key Takeaways from This Book

The Future of AI in Business

Your Next Steps

Final Thought

CHAPTER 1: INTRODUCTION TO AI AND ITS ROLE IN WEBSITES

1.1 WHAT IS AI?

INTRODUCTION

Artificial Intelligence (AI) has become one of the most transformative technologies of the 21st century, impacting industries from healthcare to finance, and now even small online businesses. For website owners, understanding AI and how it can be applied to your website is crucial for staying competitive. This lesson will give you a simple, easy-to-understand explanation of what AI is, how it works, and why it's valuable for your online business.

WHAT IS AI?

AI (Artificial Intelligence) refers to the simulation of human intelligence in machines that are programmed to think, learn, and make decisions. Essentially, AI allows computers and software to perform tasks that would typically require human intelligence, such as:

- Recognizing patterns
- Solving problems
- Understanding language
- Making decisions based on data

Unlike traditional programming, where a machine follows explicit instructions, AI uses data and algorithms to "learn" how to improve over time. For example, AI can learn to recommend products to customers based on their browsing and purchase history, similar to how a salesperson would suggest products in a physical store.

TYPES OF AI

While AI can seem like a broad and complex field, it is often divided into two main categories:
1. **Narrow AI (Weak AI):**
    - **What it is**: AI designed to perform specific tasks.
    - **Examples**: AI chatbots, recommendation systems on e-commerce websites, and email spam filters.
    - **For website owners**: Narrow AI is the most relevant and widely used. It helps you automate specific tasks such as personalizing user experiences, handling customer queries, or optimizing ads.
2. **General AI (Strong AI):**
    - **What it is**: AI that can perform any intellectual task a human can do, with the ability to think, reason, and solve new problems.
    - **Examples**: This type of AI does not exist yet and remains a concept more than a practical tool for businesses today.
    - **For website owners**: General AI is not something you'll need to worry about as it doesn't apply to daily business operations.

For your purposes, **Narrow AI** is what you'll be using. It helps improve specific areas of your website by making smarter recommendations, automating repetitive tasks, and analyzing large amounts of data to inform decisions.

HOW AI WORKS

At its core, AI relies on **data**, **algorithms**, and **machine learning** to function. Here's a simple breakdown:

- **Data**: AI needs data to learn from. For a website owner, this could include customer purchase history, product views, or user behavior on your website.
- **Algorithms**: These are sets of rules that help the AI process data and perform tasks. For example, an algorithm could tell the AI to show a user more items similar to the ones they've previously purchased.
- **Machine Learning**: A subset of AI that enables systems to learn from data without being explicitly programmed for every scenario. In other words, it improves over time as it processes more information. For example, an AI tool might start recommending better products the more users interact with your website.

APPLICATIONS OF AI IN WEBSITES

Now that you understand the basics, let's look at how AI is applied to websites like yours. Here are a few common uses:

1. **Personalized Product Recommendations**:
    - AI analyzes customer data (like browsing history and past purchases) to recommend relevant products, leading to better user experiences and higher sales.
2. **Chatbots for Customer Support**:
    - AI chatbots can answer customer queries 24/7, help users find products, and guide them through the checkout process.
3. **Content Optimization**:
    - AI can help optimize your content for SEO by analyzing the most effective keywords and content structures to rank higher in search engines.
4. **Automated Email Campaigns**:
    - AI can segment your email list and send personalized product recommendations or offers based on customer behavior, increasing open rates and conversions.
5. **Predictive Analytics**:

- AI can forecast trends based on historical data. For example, it might help you predict which products will sell well in the future, allowing you to adjust your inventory accordingly.

WHY AI IS VALUABLE FOR WEBSITE OWNERS

AI offers several benefits that can directly impact your website's success, including:

- **Time Savings**: AI automates repetitive tasks like responding to customer queries, scheduling social media posts, and generating reports.
- **Better Decision-Making**: AI tools analyze vast amounts of data and provide insights to help you make informed decisions—whether it's adjusting pricing, launching a new product, or targeting a particular audience.
- **Improved Customer Experience**: AI personalizes the customer journey by recommending relevant products, making navigation easier, and offering real-time assistance through chatbots.
- **Increased Revenue**: AI optimizes various aspects of your website—from product recommendations to ad targeting—helping to convert more visitors into customers and increasing your sales.

CONCLUSION: AI FOR BEGINNERS

AI is not as complicated as it may sound. It is a set of tools and technologies designed to make your website more efficient, personalized, and effective. Whether it's improving customer service with chatbots or driving more sales through personalized recommendations, AI can be a powerful ally in growing your website and business.

In the next lessons, we'll dive deeper into specific ways to implement AI on your website and use it to drive traffic and sales.

KEY TAKEAWAYS

- **AI (Artificial Intelligence)** is the simulation of human intelligence in machines that can perform tasks like learning, problem-solving, and decision-making.
- **Narrow AI** is the type you'll use for your website, designed to perform specific tasks like personalizing user experiences or optimizing SEO.
- AI uses **data**, **algorithms**, and **machine learning** to improve over time and become more effective at tasks.
- Applications of AI in websites include personalized recommendations, chatbots, email marketing automation, and more.
- AI helps website owners by saving time, improving decision-making, enhancing customer experiences, and increasing revenue.

1.2 THE BENEFITS OF USING AI ON WEBSITES

INTRODUCTION

As a new website owner, one of your primary goals is to grow your site, increase traffic, and convert visitors into customers. Artificial Intelligence (AI) can be a powerful tool in helping you achieve these goals by automating processes, improving customer experience, and optimizing various aspects of your website. In this lesson, we'll explore the key benefits of using AI on websites and how it can enhance your business operations, even if you're just starting out.

WHY AI IS IMPORTANT FOR WEBSITES

AI offers several advantages that can make your website smarter, more efficient, and customer-friendly. It allows you to focus on growth by automating tasks and making decisions based on real data, not just guesswork. Let's explore the main benefits AI can bring to your website:

TIME SAVINGS THROUGH AUTOMATION

One of the most immediate and obvious benefits of AI is automation. With AI, you can automate many repetitive tasks, which allows you to focus on other important areas of your business, like strategy, product development, and customer interaction. Here are some examples of how AI saves time:

- **Automated Customer Support**: Instead of manually responding to common customer questions, you can set up AI-powered chatbots that provide real-time support to your users 24/7.
- **Automated Email Campaigns**: AI tools can handle your email marketing by automatically sending personalized emails based on customer behavior, such as abandoned carts, product recommendations, or follow-up messages.
- **Social Media Posting**: AI can schedule and optimize your social media posts at the most effective times, increasing engagement without the need for constant manual intervention.

PERSONALIZATION FOR A BETTER USER EXPERIENCE

In the crowded online marketplace, offering a personalized experience can set you apart from competitors. AI can analyze user behavior, preferences, and interactions to create personalized recommendations, content, and offers for each visitor. This tailored experience leads to:

- **Higher Engagement**: Users are more likely to engage with content and products that feel relevant to their needs and interests.
- **Improved Customer Retention**: Personalized experiences create a connection between your brand and your customers, making them more likely to return and purchase again.

Example: Imagine a customer visiting your online store. AI can track their browsing history and purchase patterns to recommend products they're more likely to be interested in. This makes the customer feel understood and increases the likelihood of making a sale.

DATA-DRIVEN INSIGHTS AND BETTER DECISION-MAKING

AI can process and analyze vast amounts of data quickly, giving you actionable insights that would otherwise take hours or even days to discover manually. These insights can help you make more informed decisions, leading to better business outcomes. Key areas where AI can assist include:

- **Customer Behavior Analysis**: AI tools can analyze how visitors interact with your website—what pages they visit, how long they stay, and where they drop off. This helps you identify areas that need improvement.
- **Sales Trends**: AI can track which products are popular and predict future sales trends based on current data, helping you stock the right items and launch effective promotions.
- **Predictive Analytics**: By analyzing historical data, AI can predict future trends, such as which products will sell best during certain times of the year or how much traffic your website will receive during a campaign.

Example: You can use AI-driven analytics tools to determine why customers abandon their shopping carts. Based on this data, you could offer tailored discounts or simplify the checkout process to reduce cart abandonment.

IMPROVED MARKETING EFFICIENCY

Marketing is crucial for driving traffic and sales, and AI can optimize your marketing efforts by targeting the right audience with the right message at the right time. Here are some ways AI can boost your marketing efficiency:

- **Targeted Ads**: AI can analyze data from previous visitors and create highly targeted ad campaigns that are more likely to convert. It helps you focus your ad budget on the most relevant audiences.
- **Content Creation**: AI can assist in generating SEO-friendly content by suggesting topics based on trending keywords and what your target audience is searching for. This ensures that your content ranks higher in search engines and attracts organic traffic.
- **Optimized Ad Spend**: AI can automatically adjust your advertising budget based on real-time performance, ensuring you're not overspending on low-performing ads while maximizing ROI on effective ones.

Example: You can use AI tools to create an automated Facebook ad campaign that targets users similar to your current customers (a lookalike audience), driving traffic to your site with less effort and more precision.

ENHANCED CUSTOMER SERVICE WITH AI CHATBOTS

Customer service is a vital part of any online business, and AI chatbots can handle many of the repetitive, time-consuming tasks that come with it. Chatbots can provide instant responses to customer queries, guide users through the purchasing process, and even recommend products. Benefits include:

- **24/7 Availability**: AI chatbots work around the clock, ensuring that your customers always get assistance, even outside regular business hours.
- **Handling Multiple Queries Simultaneously**: Unlike human customer service agents, AI chatbots can handle thousands of queries at once, ensuring that no customer has to wait for help.
- **Guiding Customers to Checkout**: AI-powered chatbots can help users find the products they're looking for, offer discounts, and even assist with checkout, leading to higher conversions.

Example: A customer visits your site late at night and has questions about a product. Your AI chatbot can answer their questions, provide relevant recommendations, and even offer a discount code, leading the customer to complete the purchase without needing human assistance.

INCREASED SALES THROUGH PERSONALIZATION AND UPSELLING

AI can analyze customer behavior to recommend products they are most likely to buy, increasing your chances of making a sale. AI can also engage in upselling and cross-selling by suggesting complementary products during the checkout process.

- **Personalized Product Recommendations**: By showing products that a user is likely to buy based on their previous browsing or purchase history, AI can increase the chances of a sale.
- **Upselling and Cross-Selling**: AI can suggest upgrades or additional items that go well with the product the customer is buying, increasing the average order value.

Example: If a customer adds a piece of urban décor to their cart, AI can suggest complementary items like wall art or furniture that match their style. This increases the overall order value and gives the customer a more satisfying shopping experience.

BETTER CUSTOMER RETENTION AND LOYALTY PROGRAMS

AI can help you keep customers coming back to your website by offering personalized experiences, rewards, and follow-up interactions. Key benefits include:

- **Predictive Offers**: AI can predict which customers are likely to make repeat purchases and send them personalized offers or discounts.
- **Loyalty Programs**: AI can track customer behavior and reward them based on their purchases, engagement, or referrals, helping to build loyalty and increase repeat business.

Example: After a customer makes a purchase, AI can automatically send them a personalized thank-you email, offering them a discount on their next purchase. This small interaction can encourage the customer to return, boosting retention rates.

CONCLUSION: AI'S IMPACT ON WEBSITE SUCCESS

AI can transform your website from a simple online store to a smart, data-driven platform that understands your customers and adapts to their needs. By automating tasks, personalizing experiences, and providing insights based on data, AI helps you save time, improve marketing, enhance customer service, and increase sales. As a website owner, embracing AI will give you a competitive edge and help your business thrive in the digital marketplace.

KEY TAKEAWAYS

- **Automation**: AI helps you save time by automating repetitive tasks like customer service, email marketing, and social media posting.
- **Personalization**: AI delivers personalized product recommendations and experiences that increase engagement and sales.
- **Data-Driven Insights**: AI tools analyze customer data to help you make smarter business decisions and predict future trends.
- **Improved Marketing Efficiency**: AI optimizes your marketing efforts by targeting the right audience and adjusting ad spend based on performance.
- **Enhanced Customer Service**: AI chatbots provide 24/7 customer support, improving customer satisfaction and driving more conversions.
- **Increased Sales**: AI can boost sales through personalized recommendations, upselling, and cross-selling, leading to higher order values.

1.3 AI TOOLS FOR WEBSITE OWNERS

INTRODUCTION

As a website owner, you have access to a variety of AI tools that can help streamline your operations, enhance the customer experience, and ultimately drive more traffic and sales. The great news is that you don't need to be a technical expert to start using AI! Many AI tools are user-friendly and designed for business owners like you. In this lesson, we'll explore some of the most popular and effective AI tools for website owners, covering categories such as SEO, marketing, customer service, and personalization.

AI TOOLS FOR SEO (SEARCH ENGINE OPTIMIZATION)

SEO is critical for getting your website discovered on search engines like Google. AI tools can help you optimize your website's content, find relevant keywords, and improve your rankings without needing deep SEO expertise.

SURFER SEO

- **What it does**: Surfer SEO analyzes your website content and provides actionable recommendations to improve your rankings. It compares your pages against competitors in your niche and helps you optimize for on-page SEO factors like keyword usage, content structure, and page speed.

- **How it helps**: By using Surfer SEO, you can easily understand which keywords to target and how to improve your website's chances of appearing on the first page of Google.

CLEARSCOPE

- **What it does**: Clearscope uses AI to analyze top-ranking content for any given keyword and helps you optimize your own content to rank higher. It provides related keywords, content suggestions, and optimization tips for improving relevance.
- **How it helps**: It simplifies the process of creating high-quality, SEO-optimized content that performs well in search engines.

SEMRUSH

- **What it does**: SEMrush is an all-in-one marketing tool that uses AI to provide keyword research, competitive analysis, backlink tracking, and more. It's designed to give you insights into how your website is performing and what steps you can take to improve your SEO.

- **How it helps**: You can use SEMrush to discover new keyword opportunities, track your search engine rankings, and gain insights into your competitors' strategies.

AI TOOLS FOR CONTENT GENERATION AND OPTIMIZATION

Content is a major driver of traffic to your website, and AI tools can help you generate and optimize content that resonates with your audience while also ranking higher in search results.

JASPER (FORMERLY JARVIS)

- **What it does**: Jasper is an AI-powered content creation tool that helps you generate blog posts, product descriptions, social media content, and more. You simply provide a few prompts, and Jasper writes the content for you.
- **How it helps**: You can use Jasper to save time by automating content creation, whether it's for your blog, product pages, or marketing emails. The content is SEO-friendly, which helps improve your website's search rankings.

COPY.AI

- **What it does**: Copy.ai specializes in creating high-quality written content quickly. It can help generate marketing copy, blog ideas, product descriptions, and even ad copy based on a few inputs.
- **How it helps**: Copy.ai saves time and effort by automating the creation of professional, engaging content. This is particularly useful for generating large volumes of content for your website or marketing campaigns.

FRASE

- **What it does**: Frase uses AI to help you research, write, and optimize content for SEO. It suggests topics, outlines, and keywords based on what's performing well in your industry.
- **How it helps**: Frase assists in creating content that's not only valuable for your audience but also optimized for search engines, helping you attract more organic traffic.

AI TOOLS FOR CUSTOMER SERVICE AND ENGAGEMENT

Engaging with your visitors and offering prompt customer support are key to improving user experience and increasing conversions. AI tools like chatbots and automated support systems make this process easier.

TIDIO

- **What it does**: Tidio is an AI-powered chatbot that helps you manage customer inquiries in real-time. It integrates with your website to provide instant responses to common questions, guide customers through the sales process, and offer product recommendations.

- **How it helps**: Tidio enhances your customer service by providing 24/7 support without the need for a human team to be constantly available. This reduces response times and increases customer satisfaction.

DRIFT

- **What it does**: Drift is an AI conversational marketing platform that uses chatbots to engage with your website visitors. It helps qualify leads, schedule meetings, and answer customer questions—all in real-time.
- **How it helps**: Drift can improve customer engagement by creating personalized interactions with your website visitors, which helps convert more leads into paying customers.

LIVEPERSON

- **What it does**: LivePerson uses AI to automate customer interactions through chat, messaging, and even voice. It helps businesses engage with customers through their preferred communication channels, such as SMS, WhatsApp, or Facebook Messenger.

- **How it helps**: LivePerson's AI-driven platform enables you to handle customer queries and provide support across multiple channels, ensuring that no matter where your customers are, they can reach you.

AI TOOLS FOR PERSONALIZATION

Personalizing the user experience is a proven way to increase engagement and conversions on your website. AI tools can help you deliver a customized experience to each visitor, based on their preferences and behavior.

DYNAMIC YIELD

- **What it does**: Dynamic Yield is an AI-powered platform that personalizes website content, product recommendations, and promotions for each visitor. It collects data on user behavior and preferences to deliver personalized experiences in real-time.
- **How it helps**: By tailoring the user experience to individual visitors, you can increase engagement, improve customer satisfaction, and ultimately boost sales.

NOSTO

- **What it does**: Nosto is an AI tool that focuses on personalizing the shopping experience. It offers personalized product recommendations, pop-ups, and email marketing content based on customer behavior.
- **How it helps**: Nosto enables you to create a more relevant shopping experience, helping to drive more sales by showing the right products to the right customers at the right time.

CLERK.IO

- **What it does**: Clerk.io uses AI to create personalized product recommendations and email content based on customer activity on your website. It tracks user behavior to suggest products and offers tailored to individual customers.
- **How it helps**: With Clerk.io, you can offer personalized shopping experiences that increase conversions and encourage repeat purchases.

AI TOOLS FOR MARKETING AND ADVERTISING

AI can supercharge your marketing efforts by optimizing ad targeting, automating campaign management, and maximizing your ad spend's return on investment (ROI).

ADEXT AI

- **What it does**: Adext AI automates your digital ad campaigns by continuously optimizing ad spend and targeting based on performance. It works with platforms like Google Ads and Facebook Ads to improve results without manual intervention.
- **How it helps**: Adext AI helps you get better results from your paid ads by optimizing who sees your ads and how much you're spending, which can increase your ROI and drive more traffic to your website.

WORDSTREAM

- **What it does**: WordStream uses AI to manage and optimize Google Ads, Facebook Ads, and Bing Ads. It offers automated suggestions for improving ad performance, such as adjusting keywords, bidding strategies, and targeting.
- **How it helps**: WordStream helps you streamline your advertising campaigns by providing AI-driven recommendations that improve performance and maximize your ad budget.

REVEALBOT

- **What it does**: Revealbot is an AI tool that automates the optimization of your paid social media campaigns, particularly on Facebook and Instagram. It monitors your campaigns and adjusts bids, budgets, and targeting in real-time to improve performance.

- **How it helps**: Revealbot saves you time and increases the effectiveness of your social media ads by making real-time adjustments based on campaign performance.

AI TOOLS FOR EMAIL MARKETING AUTOMATION

Email marketing remains one of the most effective ways to engage your customers, and AI can make it even more powerful by automating and personalizing your email campaigns.

KLAVIYO

- **What it does**: Klaviyo is an AI-driven email marketing platform that helps you create personalized, automated email campaigns based on customer behavior, such as purchase history or website activity.
- **How it helps**: With Klaviyo, you can set up automated email sequences that nurture leads, recover abandoned carts, and drive repeat purchases, all while delivering highly personalized content.

MAILCHIMP

- **What it does**: Mailchimp uses AI to automate email marketing campaigns, segment your audience, and provide insights into campaign performance. It offers tools for email personalization and A/B testing to optimize your campaigns.
- **How it helps**: Mailchimp helps you deliver targeted email campaigns that are tailored to different segments of your audience, increasing engagement and conversions.

OMNISEND

- **What it does**: Omnisend is an AI-powered email marketing and automation platform designed for e-commerce businesses. It integrates email, SMS, and push notifications to create omnichannel marketing campaigns.
- **How it helps**: Omnisend allows you to automate personalized messages across multiple channels, helping you engage customers at the right time and drive more sales.

CONCLUSION: CHOOSING THE RIGHT AI TOOLS FOR YOUR WEBSITE

There are many AI tools available to help you grow your website and automate important tasks. Whether you need help with SEO, content creation, customer service, or marketing, there's an AI solution designed to make your job easier. When choosing AI tools, start by

CHAPTER 2: AI FOR IMPROVING WEBSITE TRAFFIC

2.1 USING AI FOR SEO OPTIMIZATION

INTRODUCTION

Search Engine Optimization (SEO) is crucial for getting your website noticed in search engine results, driving organic traffic, and improving your online presence. SEO can often feel complex and time-consuming, especially for new website owners. However, Artificial Intelligence (AI) has revolutionized the way we approach SEO, making it easier to optimize your website without needing to be an SEO expert. In this lesson, we'll explore how AI can help with SEO optimization, from keyword research and content creation to analyzing competitors and improving your site's ranking.

WHAT IS SEO OPTIMIZATION?

SEO optimization refers to the process of improving your website so that it ranks higher on search engine results pages (SERPs). A higher ranking increases the likelihood of users finding and visiting your website, which translates to more traffic and potential sales. Key elements of SEO optimization include:

- **Keyword Research**: Finding the right keywords that your target audience is searching for.
- **On-Page SEO**: Optimizing elements on your website such as titles, headings, meta descriptions, and content to include relevant keywords.
- **Technical SEO**: Improving the technical aspects of your website, such as loading speed, mobile-friendliness, and site structure.
- **Backlinks**: Gaining links to your website from reputable sites, signaling trust to search engines.

AI helps automate and enhance these SEO tasks, enabling you to achieve better results with less effort.

HOW AI HELPS WITH SEO OPTIMIZATION

AI-driven SEO tools use machine learning and data analysis to help you optimize your website more efficiently and effectively. Let's explore how AI assists with key SEO tasks.

AI-POWERED KEYWORD RESEARCH

Keyword research is the foundation of SEO, and AI tools can dramatically improve this process by suggesting relevant keywords that have high search volume but low competition.

TOOLS FOR AI-POWERED KEYWORD RESEARCH

- **SEMrush**: SEMrush is an AI-powered platform that provides extensive keyword research capabilities. It analyzes competitor keywords, suggests related keywords, and provides data on keyword difficulty and search volume.
- **Ahrefs**: Ahrefs uses AI to analyze top-performing keywords in your industry, providing insights into search traffic, keyword ranking potential, and competition analysis.
- **Frase**: Frase's AI-driven tool can help you discover long-tail keywords (specific phrases that users search for) that are easier to rank for but highly relevant to your target audience.

HOW AI HELPS:

- **Improves Accuracy**: AI tools analyze billions of data points across search engines to provide you with accurate keyword suggestions.
- **Identifies Opportunities**: AI can identify keyword gaps where your competitors are ranking but you're not, giving you an edge to rank for those keywords.
- **Saves Time**: AI automates the research process, saving you hours of manual work in finding and evaluating the best keywords for your content.

Example: You can use SEMrush to input a few seed keywords related to your niche (e.g., "urban décor"), and the tool will suggest hundreds of related keywords, along with data on how difficult it is to rank for each one.

2. AI-DRIVEN CONTENT OPTIMIZATION

AI can analyze top-ranking content for your target keywords and help you optimize your own content to match or exceed the competition. This includes optimizing for readability, keyword usage, and content structure.

TOOLS FOR AI CONTENT OPTIMIZATION

- **Surfer SEO**: Surfer SEO analyzes your content and compares it to the top-ranking pages for your target keywords. It provides recommendations on how to improve keyword density, word count, and other on-page SEO factors.
- **Clearscope**: Clearscope uses AI to analyze search engine results pages (SERPs) and helps you create content that is more comprehensive and relevant to what users are searching for.
- **MarketMuse**: MarketMuse leverages AI to evaluate your existing content and suggests improvements by analyzing keyword relevance, topic coverage, and competitive gaps.

HOW AI HELPS:

- **Content Analysis**: AI tools analyze competitors' content and show you exactly what you need to do to rank higher, whether it's increasing word count or incorporating specific phrases.
- **Optimization Suggestions**: AI provides real-time suggestions as you write, ensuring that your content meets the criteria search engines look for.
- **Improves User Experience**: AI ensures that your content is not only optimized for search engines but also user-friendly, helping you balance SEO with quality writing.

Example: After writing a blog post, you can use Surfer SEO to compare your content against the top-ranking pages for your target keyword. The tool will tell you how many times to include your keyword, suggest additional terms to cover, and highlight any gaps that may be preventing you from ranking.

3. AI FOR COMPETITOR ANALYSIS

Understanding what your competitors are doing right can give you valuable insights into improving your own SEO strategy. AI tools help by analyzing competitors' websites, backlinks, and SEO tactics.

TOOLS FOR AI COMPETITOR ANALYSIS

- **SEMrush**: SEMrush allows you to analyze your competitors' keyword strategies, backlink profiles, and content performance, all powered by AI.
- **Ahrefs**: Ahrefs can show you where your competitors are getting backlinks from, which pages are driving the most traffic, and what keywords they are ranking for.

HOW AI HELPS:

- **Backlink Analysis**: AI tools help you identify which sites are linking to your competitors and how you can acquire similar backlinks to boost your site's authority.
- **Competitor Benchmarking**: AI provides side-by-side comparisons between your website and competitors' sites, showing areas where you can improve.
- **Strategy Insights**: By analyzing competitors, AI can suggest which keywords and SEO tactics are most effective in your industry.

Example: If your competitor is outranking you for a particular keyword, you can use Ahrefs to discover which backlinks are helping them rank higher. You can then reach out to those sites or focus on acquiring similar backlinks to improve your own rankings.

4. AI FOR TECHNICAL SEO AUDITS

Technical SEO focuses on optimizing your website's infrastructure to ensure that search engines can easily crawl and index your content. AI tools can automatically audit your site for issues like slow page speed, broken links, and poor mobile usability.

TOOLS FOR AI-DRIVEN TECHNICAL SEO AUDITS

- **Screaming Frog**: Screaming Frog uses AI to crawl your website and identify technical SEO issues such as broken links, duplicate content, and missing metadata.
- **Google Search Console**: Google's Search Console uses AI to provide insights into how well your site is performing in terms of mobile usability, indexing issues, and page speed.

HOW AI HELPS:

- **Automated Site Audits**: AI-powered SEO tools can audit your site quickly and identify technical issues that could be hurting your search rankings.
- **Actionable Reports**: AI doesn't just point out problems—it provides suggestions for fixing them, whether it's speeding up your site or improving your mobile layout.
- **Monitoring & Maintenance**: AI tools continuously monitor your website's health, ensuring that you are alerted to any issues before they affect your SEO performance.

Example: By running an audit with Screaming Frog, you can discover any pages with missing meta descriptions or images without alt text. The tool will also highlight slow-loading pages and offer recommendations to improve load time, which can positively impact your search rankings.

5. AI FOR LINK BUILDING AND OUTREACH

Backlinks are one of the most important factors for SEO rankings. AI can streamline the process of acquiring backlinks by identifying potential link-building opportunities and automating outreach efforts.

TOOLS FOR AI-DRIVEN LINK BUILDING

- **BuzzSumo**: BuzzSumo uses AI to help you discover content that is performing well in your niche, including who is linking to it. You can use this information to create similar content and reach out to those same sites for backlinks.

- **Pitchbox**: Pitchbox automates your outreach efforts, using AI to identify relevant influencers, bloggers, and websites that may be interested in linking to your content.

HOW AI HELPS:

- **Identifying Opportunities**: AI analyzes websites in your industry and identifies those that are likely to link to your content, saving you time in manual prospecting.
- **Automating Outreach**: AI can automatically generate and send personalized outreach emails to potential backlink sources, making the process more efficient.
- **Tracking Results**: AI tools track your link-building efforts, showing you which strategies are working and which need adjustment.

Example: After publishing a high-quality piece of content, you can use BuzzSumo to find influencers and bloggers who have shared similar articles. You can then use Pitchbox to automate outreach, asking them to link to your content in exchange for valuable information.

6. AI FOR VOICE SEARCH OPTIMIZATION

With the rise of voice assistants like Siri, Alexa, and Google Assistant, optimizing for voice search has become a crucial part of SEO. AI can help you optimize your content for natural language queries and improve your chances of ranking for voice searches.

TOOLS FOR VOICE SEARCH OPTIMIZATION

- **AnswerThePublic**: AnswerThePublic uses AI to analyze what questions users are asking about specific topics, helping you tailor your content for voice search queries.
- **Frase**: Frase helps you optimize content for voice search by focusing on conversational keywords and question-based queries that are commonly used in voice search.

HOW AI HELPS:

- **Natural Language Processing**: AI tools help you identify long-tail keywords and conversational phrases that users are likely to speak into voice assistants.
- **Question-Based Content**: AI tools encourage you to create content that answers common questions users ask via voice search, increasing your chances

2.2 CONTENT GENERATION WITH AI

INTRODUCTION

Content is king when it comes to driving traffic, building brand authority, and engaging your audience online. However, producing high-quality, SEO-friendly content consistently can be time-consuming and challenging. This is where Artificial Intelligence (AI) comes in. AI-powered tools can help you generate content quickly, optimize it for search engines, and tailor it to your target audience, all while saving you significant time and effort. In this lesson, we'll explore how to use AI for content generation, covering key tools, techniques, and best practices.

WHAT IS AI-POWERED CONTENT GENERATION?

AI-powered content generation refers to the use of AI tools and algorithms to create written content based on user input, data analysis, and machine learning models. These tools can create a wide range of content, from blog posts and product descriptions to social media updates and email marketing copy.

The AI learns from analyzing vast amounts of data, including existing content, search trends, and user behavior, to generate content that resonates with readers while also being optimized for SEO. AI tools not only assist with content creation but can also enhance existing content, ensuring it ranks well on search engines and engages your audience effectively.

HOW AI IMPROVES CONTENT CREATION

AI tools offer several advantages for content generation:
- **Speed**: AI can create content quickly, allowing you to generate blog posts, articles, and marketing materials in minutes rather than hours.
- **Consistency**: AI helps you maintain a consistent content schedule, ensuring your website remains fresh and active with new content.
- **SEO Optimization**: AI tools are built to optimize content for search engines by suggesting keywords, structuring content, and improving readability.
- **Cost Efficiency**: Using AI tools for content generation can reduce the cost of hiring multiple content writers or agencies, especially for routine content tasks.

AI TOOLS FOR CONTENT GENERATION

Several AI tools can help you with content creation, whether you need blog posts, product descriptions, or social media content. Let's explore some of the most popular tools available to website owners:

JASPER (FORMERLY JARVIS)

- **What it does**: Jasper is an AI-powered content creation tool that helps you generate a variety of content, including blog posts, social media updates, emails, and more. You provide input in the form of keywords or a topic, and Jasper writes content that is SEO-friendly and tailored to your audience.
- **How it helps**: Jasper enables you to scale your content production quickly, whether you're creating long-form blog posts or short promotional content. It also provides various writing templates, including product descriptions, headlines, and ad copy, making it versatile for different needs.

COPY.AI

- **What it does**: Copy.ai uses machine learning to generate marketing copy, product descriptions, and blog content. It helps you create engaging, creative, and persuasive text based on brief prompts or key ideas.
- **How it helps**: Copy.ai is particularly useful for generating short-form content, such as email subject lines, social media captions, and ad copy. It also provides content outlines and suggestions to help guide the writing process.

WRITESONIC

- **What it does**: Writesonic is an AI-powered content generation platform that creates blog articles, landing pages, and product descriptions. It helps optimize content for SEO by suggesting relevant keywords and phrases.
- **How it helps**: Writesonic is ideal for website owners who need high-quality, SEO-optimized content quickly. It provides tools to fine-tune your content for readability, structure, and keyword optimization.

2. CREATING BLOG POSTS WITH AI

Blogging is one of the most effective ways to drive organic traffic to your website, improve your SEO ranking, and establish yourself as an authority in your industry. AI-powered tools simplify the process of writing blog posts by providing templates, outlines, and suggestions.

STEP-BY-STEP GUIDE TO CREATING A BLOG POST WITH AI

1. **Choose a Topic**:
    - Start by selecting a topic that is relevant to your audience and aligned with your website's niche. AI tools can assist by suggesting trending topics or high-traffic keywords related to your business.
    - **Example**: Using a tool like **Frase**, you can enter a broad keyword like "urban décor trends," and the AI will suggest more specific topics and questions that people are searching for online.
2. **Generate an Outline**:
    - AI can help you structure your blog post by providing a detailed outline. This outline usually includes headings and subheadings that reflect the key points or sections you should cover.
    - **Example**: Using **Jasper**, you can input your blog topic, and the tool will generate a clear outline, including an introduction, main body sections, and a conclusion.
3. **Write the Content**:

- Once you have the outline, the AI tool can generate content for each section. You can guide the AI by providing prompts or specific details, or you can let the tool create the content based on the topic.
- **Example**: You can use **Writesonic** to automatically generate each section of your blog post, including relevant keywords. It will write coherent, engaging text based on your topic and the outlined structure.

4. **Optimize for SEO**:
   - AI tools also assist in optimizing your blog post for search engines. They suggest keywords, improve readability, and ensure that the content meets SEO best practices.
   - **Example**: **Surfer SEO** can be used alongside your AI-generated content to provide recommendations on keyword usage, content length, and meta tags to ensure the post ranks higher in search results.

5. **Review and Edit**:
   - While AI tools can create a strong first draft, it's important to review and edit the content to ensure it aligns with your brand voice and adds personal insights or unique perspectives.
   - **Example**: After the AI generates your blog content, read through it, add your own insights or examples, and tweak any areas that need to reflect your personal touch or brand tone.

BENEFITS:

- **Faster Turnaround**: AI drastically reduces the time it takes to generate a high-quality blog post, enabling you to produce more content in less time.
- **SEO Optimization**: AI ensures your blog post is structured and written to maximize its chances of ranking well in search results.
- **Topic Suggestions**: AI helps you find relevant, trending topics that your audience is already searching for, increasing your content's relevance.

3. CREATING PRODUCT DESCRIPTIONS WITH AI

Product descriptions are essential for e-commerce websites. They need to be engaging, informative, and persuasive, while also containing relevant keywords for SEO purposes. AI tools simplify the process by generating product descriptions that highlight the key features and benefits of your products.

HOW AI HELPS WITH PRODUCT DESCRIPTIONS

- **Keyword Optimization**: AI tools analyze the most relevant keywords and phrases to include in your product descriptions, helping your products rank higher in search engine results.
- **Consistency**: If you have hundreds of products, maintaining consistent, high-quality descriptions can be difficult. AI ensures that your product descriptions are uniform in tone, style, and structure.
- **Persuasive Copy**: AI tools can create persuasive and compelling descriptions that highlight the benefits and features of your products, making them more appealing to potential buyers.

EXAMPLE WORKFLOW USING AI:

1. **Input Key Details**:
    - Provide the AI tool with basic information about the product, such as its name, features, benefits, and target audience.
2. **Generate a Description**:
    - Let the AI create a product description that incorporates persuasive language, relevant keywords, and a call-to-action.
3. **Optimize for SEO**:
    - Ensure the description includes SEO-friendly elements, such as product-specific keywords and relevant search terms.
4. **Edit and Review**:
    - Review the AI-generated content to ensure it aligns with your brand's tone and style. Make any necessary adjustments or enhancements.

SOCIAL MEDIA AND MARKETING CONTENT WITH AI

Maintaining an active presence on social media is key to building brand awareness and engaging with your audience. AI can help generate catchy, engaging social media posts and marketing content that resonate with your followers.

HOW AI HELPS WITH SOCIAL MEDIA CONTENT

- **Automated Content Creation**: AI tools can generate social media captions, ad copy, and promotional messages based on your target audience's preferences and engagement trends.
- **Consistency**: AI can help you maintain a consistent posting schedule by generating content regularly and even scheduling posts on your behalf.
- **Content Ideas**: AI tools provide creative content ideas, such as hashtag suggestions and trending topics, to help your posts gain visibility.

EXAMPLE WORKFLOW:

1. **Choose Your Platform**:
    - Decide which social media platform you are targeting (Instagram, Facebook, Twitter) and the type of content you want to create (promotional posts, engagement posts, etc.).
2. **Generate Captions or Posts**:
    - Use an AI tool like **Copy.ai** or **Lately** to create engaging captions, headlines, and post content.
3. **Schedule and Post**:
    - Many AI tools also allow you to schedule posts, ensuring that your content is published at the optimal times for engagement.

EMAIL CAMPAIGNS WITH AI

Email marketing remains one of the most effective ways to reach customers directly. AI can assist with email copywriting, segmenting audiences, and automating email sequences to ensure timely, relevant communication.

HOW AI HELPS WITH EMAIL MARKETING

- **Personalized Content**: AI can analyze customer data to personalize email content, including subject lines, greetings, and product recommendations.
- **Automated Campaigns**: AI helps automate email sequences, such as welcome emails, abandoned cart reminders, and post-purchase follow-ups.
- **Improved Open Rates**: AI tools can optimize subject lines and email copy for higher open and click-through rates.

EXAMPLE WORKFLOW:

1. **Set Campaign Goals**:
    - Define what type of email campaign you want to create (e.g., product promotion, abandoned cart recovery, newsletter).
2. **Generate Email Content**:
    - Use AI tools like **Klaviyo** or **Mailchimp** to generate personalized email content based on customer behavior and preferences.
3. **Review and Schedule**:
    - Review the content, make necessary adjustments, and schedule the emails to be sent at the optimal time for your audience.

CONCLUSION: AI AS A POWERFUL TOOL FOR CONTENT GENERATION

AI tools provide a significant advantage when it comes to content generation. They enable you to produce high-quality, SEO-optimized content more efficiently, whether it's blog posts, product descriptions, or social media content. AI helps website owners like you keep up with the demands of content marketing while freeing up time for other critical aspects of running your business.

KEY TAKEAWAYS:

- AI tools like **Jasper**, **Copy.ai**, and **Writesonic** can help you generate high-quality, SEO-optimized content quickly and efficiently.
- AI can assist with all types of content, including blog posts, product descriptions, social media posts, and email campaigns.
- By using AI, you can scale your content production, improve your website's SEO performance, and engage your audience more effectively.

2.3 SOCIAL MEDIA MARKETING WITH AI

INTRODUCTION

Social media is a vital marketing channel for businesses of all sizes. It helps you reach new audiences, engage with your customers, and build brand awareness. However, managing social media campaigns effectively can be time-consuming and complex, especially when you're trying to keep up with the latest trends, posting schedules, and audience engagement strategies. Artificial Intelligence (AI) can simplify this process, making your social media marketing more efficient, targeted, and impactful. In this lesson, we'll explore how AI can be used for social media marketing, covering content creation, audience targeting, scheduling, and performance analysis.

WHAT IS AI-POWERED SOCIAL MEDIA MARKETING?

AI-powered social media marketing involves using machine learning and data analytics tools to automate, optimize, and enhance your social media strategies. AI tools can assist with everything from creating engaging posts and optimizing posting times to analyzing audience behavior and improving ad targeting. By leveraging AI, you can save time, make data-driven decisions, and improve the overall effectiveness of your social media campaigns.

HOW AI ENHANCES SOCIAL MEDIA MARKETING

AI improves social media marketing in several key ways:
- **Content Creation**: AI tools can help generate and suggest content ideas, create posts, and optimize your messaging to engage your audience.
- **Scheduling and Automation**: AI platforms allow you to schedule posts at the best times for engagement and automate routine tasks like replying to comments or DMs.
- **Audience Targeting**: AI can analyze user data to target specific demographics with precision, making your campaigns more effective.
- **Performance Analysis**: AI tools can provide detailed insights into how your posts are performing, helping you fine-tune your strategy.

Let's explore how these benefits can be implemented using AI tools.

AI FOR SOCIAL MEDIA CONTENT CREATION

Creating engaging content consistently is one of the most challenging aspects of social media marketing. AI tools can assist with generating ideas, writing captions, and even designing graphics. By analyzing what has worked well in the past, AI can also help tailor your content to resonate with your audience.

TOOLS FOR AI CONTENT CREATION

- **Lately.ai**: Lately uses AI to analyze your past content and suggests the best ways to repurpose it. It creates optimized social media posts, breaking down long-form content like blog posts or podcasts into bite-sized pieces for social media.
- **Copy.ai**: Copy.ai generates captions, headlines, and ad copy for your social media channels. You can enter a few keywords or ideas, and it will provide a variety of content suggestions tailored to your brand's tone and audience.
- **Canva (AI-Powered Design Tools)**: Canva's design tools, powered by AI, help you quickly create visuals for social media posts. Canva suggests design templates and elements based on your branding and previous content, allowing you to create engaging graphics without needing advanced design skills.

HOW AI HELPS:

- **Content Generation**: AI tools generate post ideas and captions, helping you keep your content fresh and engaging.
- **Repurposing Content**: AI helps you maximize your existing content by repurposing blog posts, videos, or podcasts into multiple social media posts.
- **Visuals and Graphics**: AI-powered design tools like Canva make it easy to create high-quality visuals that match your brand's style.

Example: You can use Lately.ai to convert a recent blog post about "Urban Décor Trends" into multiple social media posts. Lately will pull key insights from the blog, create individual captions, and suggest ideal hashtags to use on different platforms.

AI FOR SOCIAL MEDIA SCHEDULING AND AUTOMATION

Timing is crucial in social media marketing. Posting at the right time can increase your engagement, visibility, and overall reach. AI tools analyze data to determine when your audience is most active and automate your social media posts accordingly. This ensures that your content is published when it has the highest chance of success, without requiring constant manual effort.

TOOLS FOR AI-POWERED SCHEDULING AND AUTOMATION

- **Hootsuite**: Hootsuite offers AI-powered scheduling that analyzes your audience's online behavior and suggests the best times to post for maximum engagement. It allows you to schedule posts across multiple social media platforms in advance.
- **Buffer**: Buffer uses AI to determine optimal posting times and automates the scheduling process. You can create a content calendar that automatically posts your content at the best times for your audience.
- **Later**: Later uses machine learning to recommend the best times for posting on Instagram, Facebook, Twitter, and Pinterest. It also provides AI-powered visual planning tools, allowing you to preview how your Instagram feed will look before posting.

HOW AI HELPS:

- **Optimal Posting Times**: AI tools analyze your audience's activity to recommend when to post for the highest engagement.
- **Automating Posts**: AI automates the process of posting content, allowing you to maintain a consistent schedule without manual work.
- **Cross-Platform Management**: AI helps you manage multiple social media platforms from one dashboard, ensuring you're present on all relevant channels.

Example: Use Buffer to schedule your posts across Instagram, Facebook, and Twitter. Buffer will analyze when your followers are most likely to engage and automatically post your content at the best times, maximizing reach and engagement.

3. AI FOR AUDIENCE TARGETING AND PERSONALIZATION

One of the biggest advantages of AI in social media marketing is its ability to segment and target your audience more precisely. AI tools can analyze user behavior, demographics, and interests to ensure your content reaches the right people. Personalized content resonates more with users and results in higher engagement rates.

TOOLS FOR AI-POWERED AUDIENCE TARGETING

- **Sprout Social**: Sprout Social uses AI to analyze your audience's behavior and suggest targeting options based on their preferences and engagement history. It helps you segment your audience into groups, allowing for more personalized content and campaigns.
- **Adext AI**: Adext uses AI to optimize your ad targeting on social media platforms like Facebook and Instagram. It automatically adjusts targeting based on real-time performance data, ensuring your ads reach the most relevant audiences.
- **Hootsuite Insights**: Hootsuite's AI-powered analytics tool provides insights into your audience's preferences, demographics, and behaviors. It helps you identify trends and refine your targeting strategy for more personalized campaigns.

HOW AI HELPS:

- **Behavioral Analysis**: AI tools analyze user data to create detailed audience profiles, ensuring that your posts and ads are seen by the right people.
- **Targeting Optimization**: AI automatically refines your audience targeting based on performance, maximizing the effectiveness of your campaigns.
- **Segmentation**: AI helps you segment your audience into specific groups based on their interests, behaviors, and demographics, allowing for more personalized marketing efforts.

Example: Use Sprout Social to segment your followers into groups based on interests, such as "Urban Décor Enthusiasts" and "DIY Home Designers." This allows you to create personalized posts and targeted ads for each segment, increasing engagement and conversion rates.

4. AI FOR SOCIAL MEDIA PERFORMANCE ANALYSIS

Tracking and measuring the performance of your social media efforts is essential to improving your strategy over time. AI tools can analyze engagement metrics such as likes, shares, comments, and click-through rates, providing you with actionable insights to optimize your campaigns.

TOOLS FOR AI-POWERED PERFORMANCE ANALYSIS

- **Sprinklr**: Sprinklr uses AI to analyze social media engagement and campaign performance. It provides insights into which types of content are driving the most engagement and offers suggestions on how to improve future posts.
- **Socialbakers**: Socialbakers leverages AI to provide detailed performance metrics and social media analytics. It helps you understand what content resonates with your audience and suggests ways to refine your strategy.
- **Hootsuite Analytics**: Hootsuite's AI-powered analytics tool measures your social media performance and offers insights into your engagement metrics, follower growth, and the effectiveness of your posts.

HOW AI HELPS:

- **Actionable Insights**: AI tools provide detailed reports on your social media performance, highlighting what's working and what needs improvement.
- **Trend Analysis**: AI identifies trends in engagement and audience behavior, helping you adjust your strategy in real-time.
- **Content Recommendations**: Based on past performance, AI tools suggest the types of content that are likely to perform best, helping you refine your content strategy.

Example: After running a campaign, use Hootsuite Analytics to analyze which posts generated the most engagement. The tool will provide insights on the best-performing content and suggest which types of posts to create more of in the future.

5. AI FOR SOCIAL LISTENING AND MONITORING

Social listening involves tracking mentions of your brand, competitors, and industry-related keywords across social media platforms. AI can help you monitor these mentions and respond to conversations in real-time, giving you insights into what your audience is saying and how you can engage with them effectively.

TOOLS FOR AI-POWERED SOCIAL LISTENING

- **Brandwatch**: Brandwatch uses AI to monitor social media conversations about your brand, competitors, and industry trends. It provides insights into how people are talking about your brand and helps you identify potential opportunities or issues.
- **Mention**: Mention is an AI-driven social listening tool that tracks mentions of your brand and relevant keywords across social media, blogs, and forums. It alerts you to important conversations and provides real-time insights.
- **Hootsuite Insights**: Hootsuite's social listening feature uses AI to track mentions of your brand, industry topics, and competitors. It helps you stay on top of conversations and respond quickly to customer feedback or emerging trends.

HOW AI HELPS:

- **Real-Time Monitoring**: AI tools allow you to track mentions of your brand in real-time, enabling you to respond to customers and engage in conversations promptly.
- **Trend Identification**: AI identifies emerging trends and topics relevant to your industry, helping you create timely content and engage with trending conversations.
- **Crisis Management**: AI can alert you to negative mentions or potential issues, allowing you to address them quickly before they escalate.

Example: Use Brandwatch to monitor mentions of your brand across social media and blogs. The AI will alert you to any positive or negative mentions, allowing you to respond promptly and engage with your audience in real-time.

CONCLUSION: AI AS A GAME-CHANGER FOR SOCIAL MEDIA MARKETING

AI tools offer powerful solutions for every aspect of social media marketing, from content creation and scheduling to audience targeting and performance analysis. By leveraging AI, you can save time, optimize your social media strategy, and create more engaging and personalized content that resonates with your audience. With the ability to automate routine tasks, analyze data, and provide real-time insights, AI is transforming social media marketing and enabling businesses to grow their online presence more effectively.

KEY TAKEAWAYS:

- **Content Creation**: AI tools like **Lately.ai** and **Copy.ai** help generate engaging social media content quickly and efficiently.
- **Scheduling and Automation**: AI platforms such as **Hootsuite** and **Buffer** analyze optimal posting times and automate the scheduling of posts.
- **Audience Targeting**: Tools like **Sprout Social** and **Adext AI** help segment and target your audience more effectively for personalized social media campaigns.
- **Performance Analysis**: AI tools such as **Hootsuite Analytics** and **Sprinklr** provide detailed insights into your social media performance and recommend improvements.
- **Social Listening**: Tools like **Brandwatch** and **Mention** use AI to track mentions of your brand and industry trends in real-time.

CHAPTER 3: AI FOR INCREASING CONVERSIONS AND SALES

3.1 PERSONALIZATION USING AI

INTRODUCTION

In today's digital world, personalization is essential for building stronger connections with your customers and enhancing their experience on your website. Personalized content, product recommendations, and communication create a more engaging and relevant experience for users, which can lead to higher conversions and customer loyalty. AI enables you to deliver personalized experiences at scale, automatically tailoring content and interactions to each user's preferences and behavior. In this lesson, we'll explore how AI can help you personalize your website, emails, and marketing campaigns to increase conversions and improve customer satisfaction.

WHAT IS PERSONALIZATION USING AI?

Personalization using AI refers to the process of leveraging machine learning algorithms and data analysis to customize the experience for each visitor. AI helps you deliver content, product recommendations, offers, and marketing messages that are tailored to the specific needs and preferences of individual users. Instead of a one-size-fits-all approach, AI allows you to offer highly targeted and relevant experiences that resonate with your audience, driving engagement and sales.

By analyzing data such as browsing history, past purchases, demographics, and user interactions, AI can predict what a customer is likely to want or do next, and then adjust your website, emails, or ads to fit their preferences in real-time.

WHY PERSONALIZATION IS IMPORTANT

Personalization is key to enhancing the user experience and driving business success for several reasons:

- **Increases Conversions**: When users see content or products that match their interests, they're more likely to take action, such as making a purchase or signing up for a service.
- **Improves Customer Retention**: Personalized experiences make customers feel valued, which encourages them to return and become loyal customers.
- **Enhances User Engagement**: Tailored content is more relevant and engaging, leading to longer sessions on your website, higher click-through rates, and more meaningful interactions.
- **Boosts Sales and Revenue**: Personalization increases the likelihood of upselling and cross-selling by recommending relevant products based on a user's preferences and behavior.

HOW AI POWERS PERSONALIZATION

AI uses various data points and algorithms to analyze user behavior and predict preferences. It then delivers real-time personalization, ensuring that each user has a unique and relevant experience. Here are some key areas where AI enhances personalization:

PERSONALIZED PRODUCT RECOMMENDATIONS

One of the most powerful uses of AI in e-commerce is personalized product recommendations. AI can analyze a user's browsing history, purchase history, and preferences to suggest products they are most likely to buy. This not only improves the customer experience but also increases average order value and conversion rates.

TOOLS FOR AI-POWERED PRODUCT RECOMMENDATIONS

- **Nosto**: Nosto uses AI to analyze customer behavior and deliver personalized product recommendations on your website and through email. It tracks user interactions and purchases to create highly relevant suggestions.
- **Dynamic Yield**: Dynamic Yield offers AI-driven personalization, including product recommendations, personalized banners, and messaging based on each visitor's browsing and purchasing patterns.
- **Clerk.io**: Clerk.io provides AI-powered personalized product recommendations in real-time. It uses machine learning to analyze customer behavior and preferences to show users the products they are most likely to purchase.

HOW AI HELPS:

- **Behavioral Analysis**: AI analyzes past interactions, such as products viewed, items in the cart, and purchase history, to deliver personalized product suggestions.
- **Real-Time Adjustments**: AI adapts recommendations in real-time based on what the user is currently browsing or searching for.
- **Upselling and Cross-Selling**: AI suggests complementary products (cross-selling) or upgraded versions of products (upselling) that increase the average order value.

Example: If a user frequently browses and purchases home décor items from your website, an AI tool like Nosto can recommend related items such as wall art or furniture, based on their past behavior. This increases the likelihood that they will add more items to their cart.

PERSONALIZED CONTENT AND MESSAGING

AI can deliver personalized content on your website, such as blog posts, videos, or articles, based on a user's interests. Additionally, AI can create personalized messaging for email campaigns, ads, and on-site notifications, ensuring that every touchpoint with your customer feels tailored and relevant.

TOOLS FOR AI-POWERED CONTENT PERSONALIZATION

- **Dynamic Yield**: Dynamic Yield allows you to personalize website content, such as banners, articles, and pop-ups, based on visitor behavior, location, and demographic data.
- **Optimizely**: Optimizely's AI-powered platform helps you create personalized experiences across your website by analyzing visitor data and adjusting content, headlines, and offers in real-time.
- **Klaviyo**: Klaviyo uses AI to personalize email marketing campaigns. It segments your email list based on customer behavior, such as browsing or purchase history, and sends targeted emails with personalized product recommendations or offers.

HOW AI HELPS:

- **Segmenting Audiences**: AI tools segment your audience based on data such as purchase behavior, interests, and demographics, allowing you to deliver personalized content that resonates with each group.

- **Dynamic Messaging**: AI delivers personalized messages on your website, emails, or ads based on user behavior, making the experience more relevant and increasing engagement.

- **Improved User Experience**: Personalizing content based on a visitor's preferences leads to a more engaging and relevant user experience, which encourages repeat visits.

Example: Suppose a customer frequently reads articles about home design trends on your website. AI tools like Dynamic Yield can highlight the latest blog posts about interior design trends when the user visits, making their experience more relevant and engaging.

3. PERSONALIZED EMAIL MARKETING

AI can significantly improve the effectiveness of your email marketing campaigns by delivering personalized content, product recommendations, and offers based on customer data. AI helps segment your audience and ensures that each user receives emails tailored to their preferences and past interactions.

TOOLS FOR AI-POWERED EMAIL PERSONALIZATION

- **Klaviyo**: Klaviyo uses AI to send personalized email campaigns based on customer behavior, preferences, and purchase history. It automates email flows, such as abandoned cart emails and post-purchase follow-ups, making them more targeted and effective.
- **Mailchimp**: Mailchimp's AI-powered tools help you segment your audience and personalize email content, ensuring that your subscribers receive relevant emails that match their interests and behavior.
- **Omnisend**: Omnisend offers AI-driven email automation that personalizes email content, such as product recommendations and dynamic offers, based on customer behavior and shopping patterns.

HOW AI HELPS:

- **Audience Segmentation**: AI automatically segments your email list based on customer behavior, such as browsing history, purchase frequency, and preferences, ensuring that each group receives relevant content.
- **Personalized Recommendations**: AI-powered email platforms recommend products and offers tailored to each recipient's interests, increasing the likelihood of conversions.
- **Automated Email Flows**: AI tools automate email sequences, such as welcome emails, abandoned cart reminders, and personalized promotions, making your email marketing more efficient and targeted.

Example: After a customer abandons their cart, Klaviyo can send an automated email reminding them about the items they left behind and include personalized product recommendations based on their browsing history.

4. PERSONALIZED WEBSITE EXPERIENCE

AI can personalize the overall website experience by customizing the layout, banners, and offers shown to each visitor. This ensures that users see the most relevant products, promotions, and content, which encourages them to stay longer and increases the likelihood of conversions.

TOOLS FOR AI-POWERED WEBSITE PERSONALIZATION

- **Monetate**: Monetate allows you to personalize every aspect of the website experience, from product recommendations and promotional banners to personalized pop-ups and offers. It uses AI to analyze user behavior and deliver real-time personalization.
- **Dynamic Yield**: Dynamic Yield personalizes website elements such as homepage banners, product categories, and even the layout, based on visitor preferences and behavior.
- **Personyze**: Personyze offers AI-powered website personalization, including personalized product recommendations, dynamic banners, and personalized content based on user behavior and demographic data.

HOW AI HELPS:

- **Dynamic Layouts**: AI can adjust the layout of your website in real-time, showing different product categories or banners based on the user's past interactions.
- **Targeted Offers**: AI displays personalized promotions and discounts to users based on their preferences and browsing history, increasing the chances of conversion.
- **Improved Engagement**: AI personalizes the user experience, making it more relevant and engaging, which encourages users to spend more time on your site and make purchases.

Example: A returning customer who has previously bought modern furniture may see a homepage banner showcasing a new collection of modern home décor, thanks to an AI tool like Monetate that personalizes the website experience in real-time.

5. PERSONALIZATION FOR RETARGETING AND REMARKETING

AI is particularly effective for retargeting campaigns, where you show personalized ads to users who have previously visited your website but didn't convert. AI tools analyze past behavior to deliver highly relevant ads that entice users to return and complete their purchase.

TOOLS FOR AI-POWERED RETARGETING

- **AdRoll**: AdRoll uses AI to create personalized retargeting ads based on users' past interactions with your website. It helps you deliver relevant ads across multiple platforms, including social media and display networks.
- **Criteo**: Criteo uses AI-powered algorithms to deliver personalized retargeting ads that encourage users to return to your site. It analyzes user behavior, such as products viewed or added to the cart, to create tailored ads.
- **Google Ads (AI Features)**: Google Ads leverages AI to optimize retargeting campaigns, automatically adjusting bids and targeting based on real-time performance and user behavior.

HOW AI HELPS:

- **Behavioral Retargeting**: AI analyzes user behavior to deliver ads that are relevant to what the customer has browsed or interacted with on your website.
- **Dynamic Ad Creation**: AI tools generate personalized ads that feature products the user has previously viewed or added to their cart, making the ad more likely to lead to a conversion.
- **Automated Optimization**: AI continuously optimizes your retargeting campaigns, adjusting bids and targeting settings to maximize your ad spend's effectiveness.

Example: A user who added items to their cart but didn't complete the purchase may see a retargeting ad from AdRoll featuring those same products, along with a personalized discount to encourage them to return and complete the purchase.

CONCLUSION: THE POWER OF AI IN PERSONALIZATION

Personalization is a key factor in improving user experience, driving engagement, and increasing conversions on your website. AI makes personalization easier, faster, and more effective by analyzing user behavior and delivering relevant content, product recommendations, and offers in real-time. Whether you're customizing your website, email campaigns, or retargeting ads, AI enables you to deliver a tailored experience to every customer, helping you build stronger relationships and grow your business.

KEY TAKEAWAYS:

- **AI for Product Recommendations**: AI tools like **Nosto** and **Dynamic Yield** personalize product suggestions based on user behavior, increasing conversions and average order value.
- **AI for Content Personalization**: Tools like **Optimizely** and **Klaviyo** deliver personalized content and messaging to website visitors and email subscribers, improving engagement and retention.
- **AI for Retargeting**: Platforms like **AdRoll** and **Criteo** use AI to create personalized retargeting ads that encourage users to return to your site and complete their purchases.
- **AI for Website Personalization**: AI tools like **Monetate** and **Dynamic Yield** adjust your website's layout, banners, and offers in real-time, providing a customized experience for every visitor.

3.2 AI-POWERED EMAIL MARKETING

INTRODUCTION

Email marketing remains one of the most effective ways to engage with your audience, nurture leads, and drive sales. However, creating and managing personalized email campaigns can be time-consuming and challenging, especially when trying to reach a large, diverse audience. This is where AI-powered email marketing comes into play. AI can help you automate, personalize, and optimize your email campaigns to ensure that your audience receives relevant, targeted content at the right time. In this lesson, we'll explore how AI enhances email marketing, the tools you can use, and the best practices for leveraging AI to improve your campaigns.

WHAT IS AI-POWERED EMAIL MARKETING?

AI-powered email marketing uses machine learning and data analysis to automate and personalize email content, subject lines, send times, and audience segmentation. AI helps marketers deliver emails that are highly relevant to individual users based on their behavior, preferences, and interactions with your website or products. With AI, you can send the right message to the right person at the right time, which increases engagement and improves conversion rates.

WHY AI-POWERED EMAIL MARKETING MATTERS

AI enhances email marketing by:
- **Personalizing Emails**: AI tailors email content to each recipient, making it more relevant and engaging.
- **Automating Campaigns**: AI can automatically send emails based on triggers, such as when a user abandons a cart or makes a purchase.
- **Improving Open and Click Rates**: By optimizing subject lines, send times, and content, AI helps you boost engagement and drive more conversions.
- **Analyzing Performance**: AI analyzes past campaigns to predict what content, timing, and strategies will work best for future campaigns.

KEY BENEFITS OF AI IN EMAIL MARKETING

AI transforms email marketing by automating and optimizing various tasks, saving you time while improving results. Here are the core benefits:

- **Personalization at Scale**: AI allows you to send highly personalized emails to thousands of recipients without manual intervention.
- **Automated Segmentation**: AI automatically segments your audience based on behavior, demographics, and preferences, allowing you to send targeted emails to the right groups.
- **Predictive Insights**: AI analyzes previous campaign data to predict which emails are most likely to resonate with each user, improving the effectiveness of future campaigns.
- **Optimal Send Times**: AI determines the best time to send emails to each recipient based on their past interactions, maximizing the chances of your emails being opened and read.
- **Dynamic Content**: AI can create dynamic content that changes based on who is receiving the email, ensuring that each user gets a personalized

experience.

PERSONALIZING EMAIL CONTENT WITH AI

Personalization is crucial for improving engagement in email marketing. AI can personalize various elements of your emails, such as the subject line, body content, and product recommendations, based on a user's behavior, purchase history, and preferences.

TOOLS FOR AI-POWERED EMAIL PERSONALIZATION

- **Klaviyo**: Klaviyo uses AI to personalize email campaigns based on customer behavior, such as purchase history, product browsing, and interaction with previous emails. It can segment your audience and tailor content to individual recipients, offering personalized product recommendations, dynamic offers, and more.
- **Mailchimp**: Mailchimp offers AI-driven tools that personalize email content and subject lines for each recipient. It uses machine learning to analyze customer behavior and deliver relevant, personalized messages.
- **Omnisend**: Omnisend allows you to create personalized email campaigns by leveraging AI to suggest products, content, and special offers based on user interactions with your website.

HOW AI HELPS:

- **Dynamic Content**: AI can automatically change the content of an email based on the recipient's behavior, ensuring that each email feels personalized.
- **Product Recommendations**: AI analyzes a user's previous purchases and browsing history to suggest products they are most likely to be interested in, increasing the chances of a sale.
- **Personalized Subject Lines**: AI tools analyze which types of subject lines resonate best with different audience segments, helping you craft subject lines that increase open rates.

Example: After a customer browses several kitchen appliances but doesn't make a purchase, Klaviyo can send an email with personalized product recommendations for kitchen gadgets, including a subject line like, "Still looking for the perfect kitchen tool?"

2. AI FOR AUTOMATED EMAIL CAMPAIGNS

AI allows you to automate email campaigns based on specific triggers or user behaviors. Whether it's sending a welcome email when someone signs up or a follow-up after a purchase, AI ensures that the right message is delivered at the right time.

TOOLS FOR AI-POWERED EMAIL AUTOMATION

- **Klaviyo**: Klaviyo automates email flows based on user actions, such as signing up for a newsletter, making a purchase, or abandoning a cart. These automated emails are personalized for each user, increasing the chances of conversion.
- **Omnisend**: Omnisend offers a robust set of AI-powered email automation tools, including workflows for welcome emails, cart abandonment, order confirmation, and post-purchase follow-ups.
- **ActiveCampaign**: ActiveCampaign uses AI to automate complex email sequences, ensuring that users receive personalized emails based on their specific actions and engagement history.

HOW AI HELPS:

- **Abandoned Cart Emails**: AI can automatically trigger emails when a customer abandons their cart, reminding them of the items they left behind and including personalized recommendations or discounts.
- **Post-Purchase Emails**: AI can automate follow-up emails after a customer makes a purchase, offering product recommendations, asking for reviews, or providing useful tips about their recent purchase.
- **Drip Campaigns**: AI helps automate drip campaigns, which are a series of emails sent over time to nurture leads or keep customers engaged.

Example: If a customer adds items to their cart but doesn't check out, Omnisend can automatically send a reminder email with the subject line, "You forgot something!" and include a discount to encourage the customer to complete their purchase.

3. AI FOR AUDIENCE SEGMENTATION

One of the most powerful ways AI enhances email marketing is through audience segmentation. AI tools can automatically group your subscribers based on behavior, demographics, and interests, ensuring that you send targeted emails to each segment. This increases the relevance of your emails and improves engagement.

TOOLS FOR AI-POWERED AUDIENCE SEGMENTATION

- **Klaviyo**: Klaviyo's AI-driven segmentation allows you to group your audience based on purchase history, email engagement, browsing behavior, and more. This helps you send tailored messages to each segment, such as loyal customers or inactive subscribers.
- **Mailchimp**: Mailchimp uses AI to segment your audience based on various factors, including demographics, purchase history, and engagement. It automatically updates these segments as users' behaviors change, ensuring that your lists are always up-to-date.
- **ActiveCampaign**: ActiveCampaign leverages AI to create dynamic segments, automatically adjusting which subscribers receive specific emails based on their behavior, preferences, and interactions.

HOW AI HELPS:

- **Behavior-Based Segmentation**: AI tools segment users based on their behavior, such as what products they viewed, how they interacted with previous emails, or how frequently they make purchases.
- **Demographic Segmentation**: AI can segment your audience based on demographics like age, location, and gender, allowing you to create more personalized and relevant campaigns.
- **Real-Time Updates**: AI automatically updates your segments in real-time, ensuring that your emails are always reaching the right people with the right message.

Example: Klaviyo can automatically segment your audience into groups like "High-Value Customers" (based on purchase frequency) and "One-Time Buyers." You can then send personalized emails to each group, offering special discounts to high-value customers and incentives for one-time buyers to return.

4. AI FOR OPTIMIZING SEND TIMES

Timing is everything in email marketing, and sending emails at the wrong time can lead to lower open rates and engagement. AI tools analyze user behavior to determine the best time to send emails to each individual recipient, maximizing the chances that they will open and interact with your message.

TOOLS FOR AI-POWERED SEND TIME OPTIMIZATION

- **Sendinblue**: Sendinblue's AI tools analyze the behavior of your email subscribers to determine the optimal time for sending emails. It customizes send times for each user, ensuring your emails arrive when recipients are most likely to engage.
- **Mailchimp**: Mailchimp's AI-powered send-time optimization feature suggests the best time to send emails based on the past behavior of your audience. It automatically adjusts send times to match user activity patterns.
- **ActiveCampaign**: ActiveCampaign's AI-driven send-time optimization analyzes user interactions and adjusts the timing of your emails to ensure they are delivered when subscribers are most likely to open them.

HOW AI HELPS:

- **Custom Send Times**: AI tools analyze when each user is most active and likely to open emails, allowing you to send emails at personalized times for maximum engagement.
- **Increased Open Rates**: By sending emails at the optimal time for each recipient, AI helps you increase your open rates and overall engagement with your email campaigns.

Example: Mailchimp analyzes when your subscribers typically engage with their emails and automatically schedules your email campaign to go out at the optimal time for each recipient, whether it's early in the morning or later in the evening.

5. AI FOR SUBJECT LINE OPTIMIZATION

The subject line is one of the most important factors in determining whether your email gets opened. AI can help optimize subject lines by analyzing which phrases, words, and structures resonate best with your audience. AI tools can even generate subject line suggestions based on previous performance data.

TOOLS FOR AI-POWERED SUBJECT LINE OPTIMIZATION

- **Phrasee**: Phrasee uses AI to generate and optimize email subject lines, predicting which words and phrases will drive the highest open rates. It uses natural language generation to create subject lines that are tailored to your audience.
- **ActiveCampaign**: ActiveCampaign's AI-driven subject line optimizer analyzes past email performance and provides suggestions for improving subject lines based on what has resonated with your audience in the past.
- **Persado**: Persado uses AI to generate and test multiple versions of email subject lines, optimizing them for engagement by analyzing past performance data and predicting what will work best.

HOW AI HELPS:

- **Subject Line Suggestions**: AI tools provide data-driven suggestions for subject lines that are likely to increase open rates, taking the guesswork out of writing engaging headlines.
- **A/B Testing**: AI tools can automatically test different subject lines and adjust future campaigns based on what performs best, ensuring continuous optimization.
- **Emotion and Tone Analysis**: AI can analyze the tone and emotion of your subject lines, ensuring they resonate with your audience's preferences.

Example: Phrasee generates multiple versions of a subject line for your next email campaign, suggesting that a more personal tone (e.g., "Here's something we know you'll love") might perform better than a generic subject line.

CONCLUSION: THE POWER OF AI IN EMAIL MARKETING

AI has revolutionized email marketing by enabling marketers to deliver personalized, automated, and highly effective campaigns at scale. With AI, you can automate routine tasks, optimize email content, and segment your audience more precisely, all of which leads to higher engagement and better conversion rates. Whether you're creating personalized product recommendations, automating abandoned cart emails, or optimizing your send times, AI helps you get more out of your email marketing efforts.

KEY TAKEAWAYS

- **Personalized Content**: AI tools like **Klaviyo** and **Mailchimp** can personalize email content based on customer behavior, ensuring each email is relevant and engaging.
- **Automated Campaigns**: Tools like **Omnisend** and **ActiveCampaign** allow you to automate email workflows, such as welcome emails, abandoned cart reminders, and post-purchase follow-ups.
- **Audience Segmentation**: AI tools can automatically segment your audience based on behavior, demographics, and preferences, ensuring your campaigns are targeted and relevant.
- **Send-Time Optimization**: AI analyzes user behavior to determine the best time to send emails, improving open rates and engagement.
- **Subject Line Optimization**: AI-powered tools like **Phrasee** can optimize subject lines to increase email open rates, ensuring your emails get noticed.

3.3 CHATBOTS AND CONVERSATIONAL AI FOR SALES

INTRODUCTION

Chatbots and Conversational AI are transforming how businesses interact with customers, especially in e-commerce and online sales. These AI-driven tools can engage with visitors in real time, answer questions, offer personalized recommendations, and even guide them through the purchasing process. By automating customer interactions, chatbots help businesses save time, improve customer service, and increase conversions. In this lesson, we'll explore how chatbots and conversational AI can boost sales, improve customer experiences, and help you automate customer support for your website.

WHAT ARE CHATBOTS AND CONVERSATIONAL AI?

A **chatbot** is a software application designed to simulate human conversation, enabling users to interact with digital devices as if they were communicating with a real person. **Conversational AI** refers to the technologies (such as chatbots or voice assistants) that enable machines to understand and respond to human language in a natural, personalized manner. In the context of e-commerce and sales, chatbots and conversational AI tools can:

- **Assist customers in real-time** with queries about products and services.
- **Recommend products** based on user behavior or preferences.
- **Provide support** during the checkout process, reducing cart abandonment.
- **Personalize conversations** to create a more engaging customer experience.

WHY USE CHATBOTS FOR SALES?

Chatbots can significantly enhance the customer experience and increase sales by providing immediate assistance, answering questions, and guiding customers through the buying process. Some key benefits include:

- **24/7 Customer Support**: Chatbots provide round-the-clock support, ensuring customers get help at any time, even when you're not available.
- **Reduced Response Times**: Chatbots can respond to customer queries instantly, improving satisfaction and reducing frustration.
- **Higher Conversion Rates**: By engaging users in real-time, chatbots can help move them through the sales funnel more quickly, leading to increased conversions.
- **Personalized Recommendations**: AI-powered chatbots analyze customer behavior to offer tailored product recommendations, which increases the chances of making a sale.
- **Lower Operational Costs**: Chatbots can handle multiple inquiries simultaneously, reducing the need for human customer service agents and lowering support costs.

HOW CHATBOTS AND CONVERSATIONAL AI BOOST SALES

Chatbots and Conversational AI can play a direct role in driving sales by guiding users through the purchasing process, offering tailored suggestions, and overcoming obstacles like cart abandonment. Here's how AI-driven chatbots can enhance your sales strategy:

PROVIDING INSTANT CUSTOMER SUPPORT

One of the main benefits of using chatbots is their ability to provide instant responses to customer inquiries. Whether a customer needs more information about a product, assistance with payment, or help navigating the website, chatbots can offer the support they need without delay.

TOOLS FOR AI-POWERED CUSTOMER SUPPORT

- **Tidio**: Tidio is an AI-powered chatbot platform that provides instant responses to customer queries. It integrates with e-commerce platforms and helps customers by answering FAQs, recommending products, and assisting with orders.
- **Drift**: Drift offers conversational AI that engages with website visitors in real time, helping them find what they need and answering questions about products or services.
- **Intercom**: Intercom combines live chat with AI automation to provide real-time support, offer product suggestions, and assist customers during their shopping journey.

HOW AI HELPS:

- **Real-Time Assistance**: AI-powered chatbots can provide immediate answers to customer questions, reducing the wait time and improving the overall experience.
- **Seamless Conversations**: AI chatbots can handle complex questions by providing step-by-step solutions or routing the query to a human agent if necessary, ensuring smooth customer service.
- **Order Assistance**: Chatbots can guide customers through the purchasing process, from product selection to payment, reducing the risk of cart abandonment.

Example: A visitor on your website is browsing various home décor items. They have a question about the materials used in one of your products. A Tidio chatbot can instantly provide the product details and even suggest related items, increasing the chances of a purchase.

2. OFFERING PERSONALIZED PRODUCT RECOMMENDATIONS

Personalization is key to increasing sales, and chatbots are excellent at delivering personalized product recommendations. By analyzing user behavior, preferences, and previous purchases, AI-powered chatbots can suggest products tailored to each customer's unique interests.

TOOLS FOR PERSONALIZED PRODUCT RECOMMENDATIONS

- **Nosto**: Nosto's AI-driven chatbots analyze customer behavior and suggest products that match their preferences. This improves customer engagement and increases the likelihood of conversions.
- **Bold360**: Bold360 provides conversational AI that delivers personalized product recommendations based on user behavior, shopping history, and preferences.
- **Clerk.io**: Clerk.io uses AI to recommend products to customers through chatbots, ensuring that each interaction is personalized and relevant to the user's needs.

HOW AI HELPS:

- **Behavioral Insights**: AI chatbots track a customer's browsing history and suggest products based on their interests, increasing the relevance of the interaction.
- **Upselling and Cross-Selling**: Chatbots can upsell by recommending premium versions of products or cross-sell by suggesting complementary items, boosting average order value.
- **Real-Time Customization**: As customers interact with your website, AI chatbots can adjust recommendations in real-time based on their actions and preferences.

Example: A customer is browsing your site for modern furniture, and a Nosto chatbot offers personalized suggestions, such as matching décor pieces or complementary furniture items. This encourages the customer to explore more products and make additional purchases.

3. REDUCING CART ABANDONMENT

Cart abandonment is a common issue in e-commerce. Chatbots can help reduce this by offering real-time support during the checkout process, reminding users about their abandoned carts, and offering incentives like discounts to complete their purchases.

TOOLS FOR REDUCING CART ABANDONMENT

- **ManyChat**: ManyChat integrates with Facebook Messenger and other platforms to engage customers who have abandoned their carts. It sends reminders and personalized offers through chat, encouraging users to complete their purchase.
- **LivePerson**: LivePerson uses AI to engage customers who are hesitant to complete their purchase by offering assistance, discounts, or answering last-minute questions in real time.
- **Gorgias**: Gorgias offers AI-powered chatbots that detect when a user has left items in their cart and send automated messages to remind them to check out, while offering personalized incentives to complete the purchase.

HOW AI HELPS:

- **Cart Reminders**: AI-powered chatbots detect when a user has left items in their cart and send timely reminders, helping to recover lost sales.
- **Incentives for Checkout**: Chatbots can offer personalized incentives, such as discounts or free shipping, to encourage customers to complete their purchases.
- **Assistance at Checkout**: Chatbots provide real-time help during the checkout process, answering questions about payment methods, shipping options, or product details that might prevent a customer from completing the transaction.

Example: A customer adds several items to their cart but leaves the site before checking out. A ManyChat bot sends a message through Facebook Messenger reminding them of their abandoned cart and offering a 10% discount if they complete the purchase within the next 24 hours.

4. COLLECTING CUSTOMER FEEDBACK

AI chatbots can be used to collect customer feedback after a purchase, allowing you to gain valuable insights into the customer experience. This feedback can help you improve your products, services, and overall user experience, which ultimately leads to higher satisfaction and more sales.

HOW AI HELPS:

- **Cart Reminders**: AI-powered chatbots detect when a user has left items in their cart and send timely reminders, helping to recover lost sales.
- **Incentives for Checkout**: Chatbots can offer personalized incentives, such as discounts or free shipping, to encourage customers to complete their purchases.
- **Assistance at Checkout**: Chatbots provide real-time help during the checkout process, answering questions about payment methods, shipping options, or product details that might prevent a customer from completing the transaction.

Example: A customer adds several items to their cart but leaves the site before checking out. A ManyChat bot sends a message through Facebook Messenger reminding them of their abandoned cart and offering a 10% discount if they complete the purchase within the next 24 hours.

4. COLLECTING CUSTOMER FEEDBACK

AI chatbots can be used to collect customer feedback after a purchase, allowing you to gain valuable insights into the customer experience. This feedback can help you improve your products, services, and overall user experience, which ultimately leads to higher satisfaction and more sales.

TOOLS FOR AI-POWERED CUSTOMER FEEDBACK COLLECTION

- **Zendesk**: Zendesk offers AI chatbots that follow up with customers after a purchase, asking them to provide feedback on their shopping experience or rate the products they bought.
- **SurveySparrow**: SurveySparrow integrates with chatbots to create conversational surveys, collecting valuable customer feedback in an engaging and user-friendly way.
- **Tars**: Tars chatbots can be programmed to collect post-purchase feedback from customers, allowing you to gather insights about their experience and make data-driven improvements.

HOW AI HELPS:

- **Real-Time Feedback**: AI-powered chatbots can ask for feedback immediately after a purchase, increasing the likelihood of getting responses while the experience is fresh.
- **Engaging Surveys**: Chatbots make the feedback process more conversational and engaging, which improves response rates compared to traditional surveys.
- **Actionable Insights**: AI analyzes feedback data to identify trends and areas for improvement, helping you refine your sales strategies.

Example: After a customer completes a purchase, a Zendesk chatbot reaches out to ask for feedback on the checkout process and product quality. The chatbot then analyzes the feedback and provides suggestions for improvements to the customer support team.

5. SUPPORTING CUSTOMERS ACROSS MULTIPLE CHANNELS

AI chatbots can support customers across multiple channels, including your website, social media, and messaging platforms like WhatsApp or Facebook Messenger. This ensures that customers can get the help they need wherever they are, improving engagement and customer satisfaction.

TOOLS FOR OMNICHANNEL CHATBOT SUPPORT

- **LivePerson**: LivePerson offers conversational AI that engages customers across multiple channels, including websites, mobile apps, social media platforms, and messaging apps like WhatsApp and Facebook Messenger.
- **Intercom**: Intercom provides AI chatbots that work across various channels, including web chat, email, and social media, ensuring consistent customer support and engagement.
- **Drift**: Drift's omnichannel conversational AI connects with users on websites, social media, and messaging platforms to ensure seamless customer service and engagement.

HOW AI HELPS:

- **Omnichannel Presence**: AI chatbots allow you to provide consistent support across different platforms, ensuring customers can interact with your brand wherever they are.
- **Seamless Integration**: AI-powered chatbots integrate with various messaging platforms, allowing you to manage all customer interactions from a single dashboard.
- **Improved Engagement**: By engaging with customers across multiple channels, AI chatbots help keep users engaged with your brand, increasing the likelihood of conversions.

Example: A customer visits your website but later has a question about their order while browsing Facebook. An Intercom chatbot seamlessly continues the conversation on Facebook Messenger, providing consistent support and helping the customer track their order.

CONCLUSION: BOOSTING SALES WITH CHATBOTS AND CONVERSATIONAL AI

Chatbots and conversational AI are powerful tools that can significantly enhance customer engagement, streamline support, and boost sales. By providing real-time assistance, offering personalized recommendations, reducing cart abandonment, and engaging users across multiple channels, AI-driven chatbots help create a more seamless and satisfying shopping experience. Whether you're looking to automate customer service or improve conversions, chatbots are an essential tool for modern businesses.

KEY TAKEAWAYS:

- **Instant Support**: AI chatbots like **Tidio** and **Drift** provide real-time assistance to customers, improving satisfaction and helping guide them through the purchasing process.
- **Personalized Recommendations**: AI tools like **Nosto** and **Clerk.io** offer personalized product suggestions based on customer behavior, increasing conversions and order value.
- **Cart Recovery**: Chatbots like **ManyChat** and **Gorgias** reduce cart abandonment by sending reminders and offering incentives to complete purchases.
- **Feedback Collection**: AI chatbots such as **Zendesk** and **SurveySparrow** collect customer feedback in real-time, providing valuable insights into the customer experience.
- **Omnichannel Support**: Platforms like **LivePerson** and **Intercom** ensure customers receive consistent support across multiple channels, improving engagement and satisfaction.

CHAPTER 4: AI FOR MANAGING AND SCALING YOUR WEBSITE

4.1 PREDICTIVE ANALYTICS AND INSIGHTS

INTRODUCTION

In today's data-driven world, businesses can leverage **predictive analytics** to make smarter, more informed decisions that drive sales, improve customer experience, and optimize operations. Predictive analytics uses historical data, machine learning, and AI algorithms to forecast future outcomes. For website owners and e-commerce businesses, predictive analytics helps anticipate customer behavior, optimize marketing efforts, and predict product demand, enabling you to stay ahead of the competition. In this lesson, we'll explore how predictive analytics works, the benefits it offers, and how you can use AI-powered tools to gain actionable insights for your website.

WHAT IS PREDICTIVE ANALYTICS?

Predictive analytics refers to the use of data, statistical algorithms, and machine learning techniques to identify the likelihood of future outcomes based on historical data. It helps businesses make predictions about customer behavior, product trends, sales forecasts, and more.

For website owners, predictive analytics can:

- **Forecast sales and demand** for specific products.
- **Anticipate customer behavior**, such as which customers are likely to purchase or abandon their cart.
- **Optimize marketing efforts** by predicting the success of campaigns and determining the best strategies to use.
- **Improve customer retention** by identifying at-risk customers and taking proactive steps to engage them.

By leveraging predictive analytics, you can make data-driven decisions that enhance business performance and increase profitability.

HOW PREDICTIVE ANALYTICS WORKS

Predictive analytics works by using historical data to identify patterns and trends, which AI and machine learning models can then use to make predictions about future behavior or outcomes. Here's how it works in practice:

1. **Data Collection**: The process begins with collecting large amounts of historical data, such as customer purchases, website traffic, marketing campaign performance, and user behavior.
2. **Data Analysis**: AI and machine learning algorithms analyze the data, looking for patterns, correlations, and trends. This analysis forms the basis for predictions about future events or actions.
3. **Model Building**: Machine learning models are built and trained using the data. These models are designed to predict specific outcomes, such as which customers are likely to buy a product or which marketing strategies will be most effective.
4. **Prediction and Insights**: Once the model is trained, it can generate predictions and insights based on real-time data. These insights help you make informed decisions to optimize your website, marketing, and customer engagement strategies.

BENEFITS OF PREDICTIVE ANALYTICS FOR WEBSITE OWNERS

Predictive analytics offers several key benefits that can help you grow your online business:

- **Improved Sales Forecasting**: Predictive analytics helps you forecast future sales, enabling you to make informed decisions about inventory, staffing, and marketing.
- **Better Customer Targeting**: You can use predictive insights to identify which customers are most likely to purchase, allowing you to focus your marketing efforts on high-value prospects.
- **Increased Customer Retention**: By predicting which customers are at risk of churning, you can take proactive steps to retain them with personalized offers or re-engagement campaigns.
- **Optimized Marketing Campaigns**: Predictive analytics can identify which marketing strategies are likely to be the most effective, helping you allocate your budget more efficiently and improve campaign

performance.

- **Enhanced Inventory Management**: Predictive analytics can forecast product demand, ensuring that you stock the right items at the right time to meet customer needs and avoid overstocking or stockouts.

PREDICTING CUSTOMER BEHAVIOR

Predictive analytics can be used to forecast customer behavior, helping you understand who is likely to buy, abandon their cart, or churn. By analyzing data such as purchase history, browsing behavior, and engagement with emails, AI-powered tools can identify patterns that indicate customer intent.

TOOLS FOR PREDICTING CUSTOMER BEHAVIOR

- **Klaviyo**: Klaviyo's predictive analytics feature helps forecast customer behavior by analyzing engagement with email campaigns, website activity, and purchase history. It predicts which customers are likely to buy again or churn, allowing you to send targeted messages.
- **Salesforce Einstein**: Salesforce Einstein offers AI-powered customer insights, helping you predict customer behavior and target the right customers with personalized offers and campaigns.
- **Optimove**: Optimove uses AI to predict customer lifetime value (CLV) and segment customers based on their likelihood to engage or make a purchase.

HOW AI HELPS:

- **Customer Segmentation**: AI tools segment customers based on their predicted behavior, allowing you to send personalized marketing messages to different groups, such as frequent buyers or customers at risk of leaving.
- **Targeted Campaigns**: Predictive models identify high-value customers who are likely to convert, enabling you to create targeted campaigns that drive sales.
- **Churn Prediction**: Predictive analytics helps identify customers who are likely to stop engaging with your brand, allowing you to take proactive measures to retain them.

Example: Klaviyo analyzes your customers' purchase history and predicts which users are most likely to make another purchase. You can then send personalized emails to those customers, offering product recommendations or discounts to encourage repeat purchases.

SALES FORECASTING AND DEMAND PLANNING

Accurately forecasting sales and predicting product demand is crucial for managing inventory and ensuring you meet customer needs. Predictive analytics can analyze historical sales data, seasonal trends, and external factors (like market conditions) to help you anticipate demand and optimize your inventory.

TOOLS FOR SALES FORECASTING AND DEMAND PLANNING

- **NetSuite**: NetSuite's AI-powered demand planning tools analyze historical sales data and predict future demand, helping businesses optimize inventory levels and improve supply chain management.
- **TradeGecko**: TradeGecko uses AI to forecast sales trends and inventory needs, enabling e-commerce businesses to anticipate product demand and avoid stockouts or overstocking.
- **Inventory Planner**: Inventory Planner provides demand forecasting tools that use predictive analytics to forecast sales trends, enabling businesses to optimize their stock levels and ordering processes.

HOW AI HELPS:

- **Sales Forecasting**: AI analyzes historical sales data and market trends to predict future sales, helping you make informed decisions about inventory, marketing, and operations.
- **Demand Planning**: Predictive analytics helps you anticipate which products will be in high demand, ensuring you stock the right items at the right time.
- **Inventory Optimization**: By forecasting demand, AI helps prevent overstocking or stockouts, reducing costs and ensuring you have enough inventory to meet customer needs.

Example: Inventory Planner analyzes past sales data for a specific product and predicts a surge in demand for the upcoming holiday season. Based on these insights, you can order additional inventory in advance, ensuring you meet customer demand and maximize sales.

OPTIMIZING MARKETING CAMPAIGNS

Predictive analytics can help you optimize your marketing efforts by identifying which campaigns are most likely to succeed, which channels perform best, and which audiences are most receptive to your messages. This enables you to allocate your marketing budget more efficiently and improve overall campaign performance.

TOOLS FOR PREDICTIVE MARKETING INSIGHTS

- **HubSpot**: HubSpot uses predictive analytics to analyze your marketing campaigns and suggest optimizations based on past performance. It identifies which channels, content types, and messaging are most effective for engaging your audience.
- **Marketo**: Marketo's AI-powered marketing platform provides predictive insights into which campaigns will drive the best results, helping you refine your marketing strategy and target the right audiences.
- **AdRoll**: AdRoll's predictive marketing tools analyze user behavior and campaign performance to help you identify which advertising strategies will be most effective in reaching your audience.

HOW AI HELPS:

- **Campaign Effectiveness**: AI tools analyze the performance of past campaigns and predict which strategies are most likely to generate high engagement and conversions.
- **Channel Optimization**: Predictive analytics identify which marketing channels (email, social media, paid ads) are most effective for reaching your target audience, helping you optimize your marketing spend.
- **Audience Targeting**: AI-powered tools segment your audience based on predicted behavior, ensuring your campaigns are delivered to the users most likely to engage or convert.

Example: HubSpot analyzes the performance of your email campaigns and identifies that promotional emails sent on Wednesdays have the highest open rates. Based on this insight, you adjust your email schedule to send future promotions on Wednesdays to maximize engagement.

ENHANCING CUSTOMER RETENTION

Retaining existing customers is often more cost-effective than acquiring new ones. Predictive analytics can help you identify customers at risk of churning and develop strategies to re-engage them before they leave. By analyzing factors like purchase frequency, engagement levels, and customer satisfaction, AI-powered tools can predict which customers need attention and what actions to take.

TOOLS FOR PREDICTING CUSTOMER RETENTION

- **Custora**: Custora's AI-driven platform predicts which customers are at risk of churning and offers insights into how to retain them. It helps you identify segments of customers who need re-engagement campaigns.
- **Optimove**: Optimove's predictive models analyze customer behavior to identify at-risk customers and suggest personalized offers or incentives to keep them engaged.
- **Salesforce Einstein**: Salesforce Einstein provides AI-powered customer retention insights, helping businesses predict which customers are likely to churn and take proactive steps to retain them.

HOW AI HELPS:

- **Churn Prediction**: AI models identify customers who are at risk of leaving based on factors like declining engagement, purchase frequency, or support interactions.

- **Proactive Engagement**: Predictive analytics enables you to take action before customers churn by offering personalized incentives, discounts, or loyalty rewards.

- **Retention Campaigns**: AI suggests re-engagement strategies, such as tailored email campaigns or targeted ads, to win back at-risk customers.

Example: Optimove identifies a segment of customers who haven't made a purchase in the past 60 days. You create a personalized re-engagement email campaign offering a discount on their next purchase, helping to retain these customers and encourage them to return.

PRICING OPTIMIZATION

AI-powered predictive analytics can help you optimize pricing strategies by analyzing market trends, customer behavior, and competitor pricing. This allows you to dynamically adjust prices based on demand, maximizing both sales and profitability.

TOOLS FOR PRICING OPTIMIZATION

- **Prisync**: Prisync's AI-driven pricing tool analyzes competitor prices and market demand, helping businesses dynamically adjust their prices to remain competitive while maximizing profits.
- **Wiser**: Wiser provides predictive pricing insights, allowing businesses to optimize their pricing strategies based on real-time market trends, customer demand, and competitor pricing.
- **Competera**: Competera uses AI to analyze historical pricing data and competitor trends, helping businesses set the optimal price for their products to maximize sales and profitability.

HOW AI HELPS:

- **Dynamic Pricing**: AI tools adjust prices in real time based on demand, market conditions, and competitor prices, helping you stay competitive and increase sales.

- **Profit Optimization**: Predictive analytics identify the best price points for maximizing both sales and profitability, ensuring you strike the right balance between volume and margins.

- **Price Sensitivity**: AI analyzes customer behavior to understand how price changes affect demand, allowing you to set prices that appeal to your target audience without sacrificing profitability.

Example: Prisync analyzes competitor pricing and market demand for a popular product on your website. Based on these insights, you adjust the price to remain competitive while maximizing your profit margin, leading to increased sales.

CONCLUSION: LEVERAGING PREDICTIVE ANALYTICS FOR BUSINESS GROWTH

Predictive analytics is a powerful tool for website owners and e-commerce businesses, offering valuable insights into customer behavior, sales trends, and marketing effectiveness. By leveraging AI-powered tools, you can make data-driven decisions that improve customer retention, optimize marketing campaigns, forecast demand, and drive overall business growth. Whether you're predicting which products will sell, identifying at-risk customers, or optimizing your pricing strategy, predictive analytics helps you stay ahead of the competition and maximize profitability.

KEY TAKEAWAYS:

- **Customer Behavior Prediction**: AI-powered tools like **Klaviyo** and **Salesforce Einstein** can predict customer behavior, helping you identify high-value customers, target at-risk users, and drive conversions.
- **Sales Forecasting**: Tools like **NetSuite** and **Inventory Planner** use predictive analytics to forecast sales trends and optimize inventory management.
- **Marketing Optimization**: AI-driven platforms like **HubSpot** and **Marketo** provide predictive insights that help refine your marketing campaigns and improve audience targeting.
- **Customer Retention**: Predictive analytics tools like **Custora** and **Optimove** identify customers at risk of churning and suggest proactive strategies to retain them.
- **Pricing Optimization**: AI tools like **Prisync** and **Competera** enable dynamic pricing strategies based on market demand, competitor prices, and customer behavior.

4.2 AI FOR DYNAMIC PRICING AND PROMOTIONS

INTRODUCTION

Pricing and promotions play a crucial role in attracting customers, boosting sales, and maintaining a competitive edge in the marketplace. However, determining the optimal price for your products or offering the right promotions at the right time can be challenging. That's where **AI-powered dynamic pricing and promotions** come in. Dynamic pricing allows businesses to adjust prices in real time based on factors like demand, competition, and customer behavior. With AI, you can optimize pricing strategies and promotions to maximize sales, improve profitability, and offer personalized discounts to your customers. In this lesson, we'll explore how AI-driven dynamic pricing works, the tools you can use, and how to implement AI-powered promotions to enhance your online business.

WHAT IS DYNAMIC PRICING?

Dynamic pricing is a pricing strategy where the price of a product or service is continuously adjusted based on real-time data such as supply, demand, competitor prices, and market trends. AI-powered dynamic pricing tools use machine learning algorithms and predictive analytics to determine the most effective prices for maximizing sales and profitability. This allows businesses to remain competitive and responsive to market conditions without manually adjusting prices.

For example, online marketplaces like Amazon use dynamic pricing to adjust product prices multiple times a day based on demand, competitor prices, and other market factors. AI makes this process automated and more precise, ensuring that pricing is optimized in real time.

WHAT ARE AI-POWERED PROMOTIONS?

AI-powered promotions use data and machine learning to offer personalized discounts, deals, or incentives to customers based on their behavior, preferences, and past purchases. AI analyzes customer data to predict which promotions will be most effective for specific users, helping businesses boost engagement, improve conversion rates, and increase customer loyalty.

HOW AI IMPROVES DYNAMIC PRICING AND PROMOTIONS

AI brings significant advantages to pricing and promotional strategies by making them more efficient, responsive, and personalized. Key benefits include:

- **Real-Time Adjustments**: AI can automatically adjust prices and promotions in real time based on factors like demand, competitor activity, and customer behavior.
- **Increased Sales and Profitability**: Dynamic pricing helps you find the optimal price point to maximize both sales volume and profit margins.
- **Personalized Offers**: AI can deliver personalized promotions and discounts to customers based on their purchase history and behavior, increasing the likelihood of conversion.
- **Competitive Advantage**: AI helps you stay competitive by constantly monitoring and adjusting prices based on market trends and competitor pricing.
- **Reduced Manual Effort**: AI automates pricing and promotional adjustments, reducing the need for manual interventions and helping businesses

operate more efficiently.

DYNAMIC PRICING WITH AI

AI-powered dynamic pricing systems continuously analyze data such as competitor pricing, market demand, customer behavior, and seasonal trends to determine the optimal price for your products. This ensures that you can maximize sales and profits by offering the right price at the right time.

TOOLS FOR AI-POWERED DYNAMIC PRICING

- **Prisync**: Prisync is an AI-powered dynamic pricing tool that tracks competitor prices and market trends to help businesses adjust their prices in real time. It ensures that your prices remain competitive while optimizing profit margins.
- **Competera**: Competera uses AI and machine learning to provide dynamic pricing recommendations based on demand, competitors, and customer willingness to pay. It helps e-commerce businesses optimize prices to drive sales while maintaining profitability.
- **Intelligems**: Intelligems uses AI-driven pricing models to dynamically adjust prices based on real-time market conditions, such as competitor pricing and customer demand patterns. It provides insights into the impact of different pricing strategies.

HOW AI HELPS:

- **Real-Time Adjustments**: AI dynamically adjusts product prices based on market trends, competitor activity, and customer demand, ensuring that your prices remain competitive and optimized for sales.
- **Maximizing Profit Margins**: AI analyzes historical data to predict the price points that will maximize both sales and profits, ensuring you strike the right balance between affordability and profitability.
- **Demand Prediction**: AI uses predictive analytics to forecast customer demand and adjust prices accordingly, preventing stockouts during high-demand periods and avoiding overpricing during low-demand periods.

Example: Prisync monitors your competitors' prices and sees that a competing product has dropped in price. The AI automatically adjusts your price to remain competitive while maintaining your profit margin, helping you stay ahead in the market.

AI-POWERED PROMOTIONS AND DISCOUNTS

Promotions and discounts are essential tools for boosting sales, especially during seasonal campaigns or when trying to move inventory. AI-powered promotions allow you to tailor discounts to individual customers based on their preferences, behavior, and buying patterns. This personalization makes promotions more effective and improves customer engagement.

TOOLS FOR AI-POWERED PROMOTIONS

- **Dynamic Yield**: Dynamic Yield uses AI to create personalized promotions based on customer behavior, such as offering discounts to first-time buyers or providing targeted offers based on browsing history.
- **Fidel API**: Fidel offers AI-powered promotions by analyzing customer transactions and providing tailored rewards and offers based on their purchase history, helping increase customer loyalty and engagement.
- **LoyaltyLion**: LoyaltyLion integrates AI-driven promotions with your loyalty program, offering personalized discounts, rewards, and incentives to customers based on their activity and interactions with your brand.

HOW AI HELPS:

- **Personalized Discounts**: AI analyzes customer data, such as past purchases and browsing behavior, to offer personalized discounts that are more likely to lead to conversions.
- **Targeted Promotions**: AI-powered tools segment customers based on their behavior and purchasing patterns, ensuring that promotions are relevant and timely. For example, frequent shoppers might receive loyalty rewards, while first-time visitors might get a welcome discount.
- **Optimized Timing**: AI determines the best time to offer promotions based on customer activity, ensuring that discounts are offered when customers are most likely to make a purchase.

Example: Dynamic Yield identifies a customer who has been browsing your furniture category multiple times without making a purchase. The AI-powered tool sends them a personalized promotion offering 10% off furniture, increasing the likelihood of conversion.

OPTIMIZING INVENTORY AND DEMAND WITH DYNAMIC PRICING

AI can help you optimize your inventory by adjusting prices based on demand forecasts. For example, when AI predicts high demand for a particular product, it can raise the price to capitalize on the increased interest. Conversely, when demand is low or when you need to move excess inventory, AI can trigger discounts to stimulate sales.

TOOLS FOR INVENTORY AND DEMAND OPTIMIZATION

- **Clear Demand**: Clear Demand's AI-powered tools analyze inventory levels and market demand to dynamically adjust prices, ensuring optimal sales and profitability. It helps retailers manage promotions and optimize inventory turnover.
- **Inventory Planner**: Inventory Planner uses AI to predict demand for products and recommend pricing strategies that align with inventory levels, helping you manage stock efficiently.

HOW AI HELPS:

- **Demand-Based Pricing**: AI adjusts prices in real time based on demand forecasts, allowing you to capitalize on high-demand periods or clear out low-demand products with discounts.

- **Inventory Optimization**: AI ensures that your pricing strategy aligns with your inventory needs, helping you sell products at the right time to avoid overstocking or stockouts.

- **Revenue Maximization**: By optimizing pricing based on inventory levels, AI helps maximize revenue, especially during peak sales periods or when clearing out old inventory.

Example: Inventory Planner forecasts high demand for a seasonal product and recommends increasing the price to maximize profits during the peak season. Once demand drops, the tool suggests lowering the price or offering a discount to move the remaining inventory.

PERSONALIZED PRICING FOR DIFFERENT CUSTOMER SEGMENTS

AI allows businesses to offer personalized pricing and promotions to different customer segments based on their behavior, demographics, and purchase history. This ensures that each customer receives a tailored experience that maximizes the likelihood of conversion.

TOOLS FOR PERSONALIZED PRICING

- **Personyze**: Personyze uses AI to deliver personalized pricing and promotions to different customer segments based on their behavior and interaction with your website. It offers dynamic pricing and discounts tailored to each user.

- **Qubit**: Qubit uses AI-driven personalization to create individualized offers and pricing based on customer data, such as their purchase history, location, and browsing patterns.

HOW AI HELPS:

- **Segmented Pricing**: AI segments customers based on their purchasing behavior and offers personalized prices or promotions to encourage higher conversion rates.
- **Tailored Offers**: AI delivers tailored discounts and incentives to specific customer groups, such as offering VIP customers exclusive deals or providing new visitors with welcome offers.
- **Increased Engagement**: By offering personalized pricing, AI helps increase customer engagement and loyalty, as customers feel they are receiving offers that cater to their needs.

Example: Personyze segments your audience into frequent buyers, first-time visitors, and inactive customers. Each segment receives a personalized pricing offer—loyal customers might get a bulk discount, while first-time visitors are offered a 15% discount on their first purchase.

COMPETITOR MONITORING AND PRICE MATCHING

AI-powered dynamic pricing tools can monitor competitor prices in real time and automatically adjust your prices to match or beat competitors. This helps you stay competitive in the marketplace and ensures that your prices are always optimized for the current market conditions.

TOOLS FOR COMPETITOR MONITORING AND PRICE MATCHING

- **Wiser**: Wiser's AI-driven pricing platform monitors competitor prices in real time and adjusts your prices accordingly. It helps e-commerce businesses stay competitive by offering price-matching capabilities and optimized pricing strategies.
- **Competera**: Competera uses AI to monitor market trends and competitor prices, offering dynamic price adjustments that keep your business competitive while maximizing profitability.

HOW AI HELPS:

- **Real-Time Competitor Monitoring**: AI tools track competitor pricing in real time and automatically adjust your prices to remain competitive.
- **Price Matching**: AI-powered platforms can automatically match or beat competitor prices, ensuring that your products remain attractive to customers without sacrificing profitability.
- **Market Trend Analysis**: AI tools analyze broader market trends and suggest pricing strategies that align with the competitive landscape.

Example: Wiser monitors your competitors' prices and sees that a similar product is being sold at a 5% lower price. The AI system automatically adjusts your price to match, helping you stay competitive while maintaining your margins.

TESTING AND ANALYZING PRICING STRATEGIES

AI can also help you test and analyze different pricing strategies to determine which ones are most effective for your business. Through A/B testing and predictive analytics, AI tools provide insights into how price changes impact customer behavior, conversions, and profitability.

TOOLS FOR TESTING PRICING STRATEGIES

- **Intelligems**: Intelligems allows businesses to run A/B tests on different pricing strategies to see how customers respond. It uses AI to analyze the results and recommend the optimal pricing strategy based on real-time data.
- **Dynamic Pricing by Omnia Retail**: Omnia's dynamic pricing tool helps businesses test and analyze pricing strategies to determine which approaches generate the highest sales and profits.

HOW AI HELPS:

- **A/B Testing**: AI-powered tools enable you to run tests on different pricing strategies, comparing how price changes affect sales, conversion rates, and customer satisfaction.

- **Data-Driven Decisions**: AI analyzes the results of pricing tests to recommend the optimal pricing strategy, ensuring that you make data-driven decisions.

- **Continuous Optimization**: AI continuously monitors the effectiveness of your pricing strategies, allowing you to adjust in real time based on customer response and market conditions.

Example: Intelligems runs an A/B test on two different pricing strategies for a new product—one with a 10% discount and one with a free shipping offer. The AI tool analyzes customer responses and determines that the free shipping offer leads to higher conversions, suggesting it as the preferred strategy.

CONCLUSION: USING AI FOR DYNAMIC PRICING AND PROMOTIONS

AI-powered dynamic pricing and promotions offer a powerful way to optimize your sales strategy by adjusting prices in real time, offering personalized promotions, and responding to market conditions. By leveraging AI tools, businesses can ensure they remain competitive, maximize profits, and offer personalized experiences to their customers. Whether you're optimizing inventory, testing pricing strategies, or offering tailored discounts, AI can help you make smarter decisions and drive higher sales.

KEY TAKEAWAYS:

- **Dynamic Pricing**: AI tools like **Prisync** and **Competera** allow you to adjust prices in real time based on demand, competition, and market trends, maximizing profitability and sales.
- **AI-Powered Promotions**: Tools like **Dynamic Yield** and **Fidel API** use AI to deliver personalized promotions and discounts that drive conversions and improve customer engagement.
- **Inventory Optimization**: AI-powered tools help align pricing with demand and inventory levels, ensuring that you optimize stock management and revenue.
- **Personalized Pricing**: Platforms like **Personyze** offer personalized pricing and discounts to different customer segments, increasing engagement and conversions.
- **Competitor Monitoring**: AI tools like **Wiser** and **Competera** monitor competitor prices and adjust your prices accordingly, ensuring you remain competitive.

4.3 AI FOR CUSTOMER RETENTION

INTRODUCTION

Customer retention is one of the most critical aspects of running a successful business. While acquiring new customers is essential, keeping existing customers is often more cost-effective and leads to higher lifetime value. By leveraging **AI for customer retention**, you can predict which customers are at risk of leaving, personalize re-engagement strategies, and build stronger loyalty over time. AI tools help businesses identify early signs of churn, deliver personalized offers to retain customers, and improve overall customer satisfaction. In this lesson, we'll explore how AI can help with customer retention, the tools you can use, and best practices for implementing AI-powered retention strategies.

WHAT IS CUSTOMER RETENTION?

Customer retention refers to the strategies and actions businesses take to keep existing customers and encourage repeat purchases. It involves understanding customer behavior, providing personalized experiences, and proactively addressing potential issues that may cause a customer to stop engaging with your brand. Effective customer retention improves customer loyalty and reduces churn, leading to a higher customer lifetime value (CLV).

WHY USE AI FOR CUSTOMER RETENTION?

AI is a game-changer for customer retention because it helps businesses:

- **Predict Customer Churn**: AI can analyze customer behavior and identify patterns that suggest a customer is at risk of leaving, allowing you to take proactive steps to retain them.
- **Personalize Engagement**: AI can deliver personalized re-engagement campaigns, offers, and messages tailored to individual customers, increasing the likelihood of retention.
- **Improve Customer Satisfaction**: AI helps businesses identify and address customer pain points, ensuring that customers have a positive experience and remain loyal.
- **Automate Retention Campaigns**: AI can automate retention efforts, such as sending personalized emails, offers, or loyalty rewards, based on customer activity and behavior.

By integrating AI into your retention strategy, you can create more effective, personalized experiences that build long-term customer relationships and reduce churn.

HOW AI HELPS WITH CUSTOMER RETENTION

AI improves customer retention through predictive analytics, personalized communication, automated re-engagement strategies, and more. Here are the main ways AI can help:

PREDICTING CUSTOMER CHURN WITH AI

One of the most powerful uses of AI in customer retention is predicting which customers are at risk of leaving. By analyzing past behavior, such as purchase frequency, engagement levels, and support interactions, AI can identify patterns that indicate a customer may churn. With this information, you can take proactive measures to retain those customers.

TOOLS FOR PREDICTING CUSTOMER CHURN

- **Optimove**: Optimove uses predictive analytics to identify customers at risk of churn by analyzing customer behavior, purchase patterns, and engagement data. It helps businesses create personalized re-engagement campaigns to retain those customers.
- **Custora**: Custora's AI-driven platform predicts which customers are likely to churn based on data such as order history, browsing behavior, and customer satisfaction. It provides insights into the best actions to take to retain those customers.
- **Salesforce Einstein**: Salesforce Einstein uses AI to predict customer churn by analyzing customer interactions and engagement data. It helps businesses identify churn risks and take proactive steps to re-engage those customers.

HOW AI HELPS:

- **Churn Risk Identification**: AI models analyze various data points to predict which customers are most likely to stop engaging with your brand.
- **Proactive Retention**: By identifying at-risk customers early, businesses can offer personalized incentives or targeted campaigns to prevent churn.
- **Behavioral Insights**: AI tools provide insights into customer behavior trends that may lead to churn, helping you address potential issues before they escalate.

Example: Optimove analyzes a segment of customers who haven't made a purchase in the last 90 days and predicts which of these customers are likely to churn. Based on these insights, you can launch a targeted email campaign offering a special discount to re-engage those customers.

PERSONALIZED RE-ENGAGEMENT CAMPAIGNS

Once AI identifies customers at risk of churn, the next step is re-engagement. AI tools can help you create personalized re-engagement campaigns that offer incentives, tailored content, or personalized offers to encourage customers to return. These campaigns are more effective than generic messages because they are based on the specific behavior and preferences of each customer.

TOOLS FOR AI-POWERED RE-ENGAGEMENT

- **Klaviyo**: Klaviyo uses AI to personalize re-engagement campaigns by sending targeted emails to customers based on their behavior, such as product recommendations or exclusive discounts.
- **ActiveCampaign**: ActiveCampaign offers AI-powered re-engagement campaigns that automatically send personalized messages to customers who have become inactive or are at risk of churning.
- **HubSpot**: HubSpot uses AI to create re-engagement workflows, delivering personalized content and offers to customers who haven't interacted with your brand recently, encouraging them to come back.

HOW AI HELPS:

- **Targeted Campaigns**: AI segments customers based on behavior and creates personalized offers or messages that resonate with their interests, improving the likelihood of re-engagement.
- **Automated Re-Engagement**: AI-powered tools automate re-engagement efforts, ensuring that customers receive timely and relevant offers without manual intervention.
- **Data-Driven Personalization**: AI analyzes customer data to recommend personalized offers, discounts, or products that are most likely to entice the customer to return.

Example: Klaviyo detects a customer who has abandoned their cart twice in the last month without making a purchase. It sends a personalized email offering a 15% discount on the items in the cart, encouraging the customer to complete the purchase.

LOYALTY PROGRAMS POWERED BY AI

Loyalty programs are a proven way to retain customers, and AI can take these programs to the next level by personalizing rewards and incentives based on customer behavior and preferences. AI can track customer engagement, purchase frequency, and other metrics to deliver tailored loyalty rewards that keep customers coming back.

TOOLS FOR AI-DRIVEN LOYALTY PROGRAMS

- **LoyaltyLion**: LoyaltyLion uses AI to create personalized loyalty programs that reward customers based on their activity, purchase history, and interactions with your brand. The platform allows you to deliver customized rewards and incentives that increase customer engagement.
- **Smile.io**: Smile.io offers AI-powered loyalty programs that reward customers for specific actions, such as making a purchase, writing a review, or referring a friend. The platform personalizes rewards based on customer behavior, ensuring that each customer feels valued.
- **Yotpo**: Yotpo's AI-driven loyalty platform tracks customer behavior and engagement to deliver personalized rewards and loyalty points, increasing customer satisfaction and retention.

HOW AI HELPS:

- **Personalized Rewards**: AI analyzes customer activity and preferences to deliver personalized rewards that are relevant to each customer, making loyalty programs more engaging and effective.
- **Behavior-Based Incentives**: AI tracks customer behavior, such as purchase frequency or referral activity, and delivers rewards based on those actions, encouraging repeat business.
- **Automated Loyalty Management**: AI-powered tools automate the management of loyalty programs, ensuring that customers receive timely rewards and incentives without manual intervention.

Example: LoyaltyLion tracks a customer who frequently purchases from your site but hasn't engaged with your loyalty program. The AI recommends offering double loyalty points for their next purchase to encourage more engagement with the program, increasing their chances of becoming a repeat customer.

CUSTOMER FEEDBACK AND SENTIMENT ANALYSIS

Understanding customer sentiment is key to retaining them. AI can analyze customer feedback and reviews, identifying pain points or issues that need to be addressed to improve the customer experience. By tracking customer sentiment in real time, AI tools help businesses respond proactively, ensuring that customers are satisfied and remain loyal.

TOOLS FOR AI-POWERED SENTIMENT ANALYSIS

- **Zendesk**: Zendesk's AI-powered customer support platform includes sentiment analysis, which monitors customer feedback, reviews, and support interactions to identify areas where the customer experience can be improved.
- **Medallia**: Medallia uses AI to analyze customer feedback and reviews, identifying sentiment trends and providing insights into customer satisfaction and potential issues that could lead to churn.
- **Clarabridge**: Clarabridge offers AI-driven sentiment analysis that tracks customer conversations, reviews, and social media mentions to gauge customer satisfaction and uncover potential retention issues.

HOW AI HELPS:

- **Real-Time Sentiment Tracking**: AI tools analyze customer feedback and reviews in real time, helping you identify negative sentiment and address it before it leads to churn.
- **Actionable Insights**: AI-powered sentiment analysis provides actionable insights into customer satisfaction, highlighting areas where improvements can be made to enhance the customer experience.
- **Proactive Issue Resolution**: AI helps you detect potential issues early, allowing you to address customer concerns before they escalate into dissatisfaction or churn.

Example: Zendesk monitors customer support tickets and detects a negative sentiment in feedback from a particular customer. The system automatically flags the issue and suggests sending a personalized follow-up email to resolve the problem and improve the customer's experience.

AUTOMATING RETENTION EFFORTS WITH AI

AI can automate many aspects of your retention strategy, from sending personalized emails to delivering loyalty rewards. By automating retention efforts, you can ensure that customers are consistently engaged without requiring manual intervention, freeing up time for your team to focus on more complex tasks.

TOOLS FOR AI-POWERED RETENTION AUTOMATION

- **ActiveCampaign**: ActiveCampaign automates retention workflows, such as sending personalized re-engagement emails or loyalty offers, based on customer behavior. The platform uses AI to ensure that retention efforts are timely and relevant.
- **HubSpot**: HubSpot's AI-powered automation tools allow businesses to create automated retention campaigns, delivering personalized content and offers to customers who haven't interacted with the brand recently.
- **Klaviyo**: Klaviyo automates re-engagement campaigns and loyalty rewards, sending personalized offers and incentives to customers who are at risk of churning or have become inactive.

HOW AI HELPS:

- **Automated Campaigns**: AI automates the process of sending personalized retention emails, offers, and rewards based on customer activity, ensuring consistent engagement.
- **Trigger-Based Actions**: AI uses behavioral triggers to send retention-focused communications, such as discounts for inactive customers or loyalty rewards for frequent shoppers.
- **Scalable Retention**: AI allows businesses to scale their retention efforts without requiring manual effort, ensuring that every customer receives timely and relevant communication.

Example: ActiveCampaign automates a retention workflow that sends personalized offers to customers who haven't made a purchase in the past 60 days. The AI tool also tracks engagement with the emails, adjusting future campaigns based on customer response.

IMPROVING THE CUSTOMER EXPERIENCE WITH AI

AI can enhance the overall customer experience by providing personalized interactions, timely support, and tailored recommendations. By improving the customer experience, AI helps businesses increase customer satisfaction and build long-term loyalty.

TOOLS FOR ENHANCING THE CUSTOMER EXPERIENCE

- **Intercom**: Intercom's AI-powered chatbots provide personalized customer support and product recommendations, improving the overall customer experience and encouraging repeat business.
- **Tidio**: Tidio offers AI-driven chatbots that assist customers in real time, providing instant responses to inquiries and helping guide customers through the purchasing process, which improves satisfaction and retention.
- **Zendesk**: Zendesk's AI-powered support platform improves the customer experience by automating responses to common queries, providing instant support, and analyzing customer interactions to identify areas for improvement.

HOW AI HELPS:

- **Personalized Support**: AI-powered chatbots and customer support tools provide personalized assistance, improving the customer experience and ensuring that customers feel valued.
- **Instant Responses**: AI tools deliver instant responses to customer inquiries, reducing wait times and increasing satisfaction.
- **Proactive Engagement**: AI can proactively engage with customers, offering support or product recommendations before they even ask, improving the overall experience.

Example: A customer visits your website with questions about a product. A Tidio chatbot offers instant assistance, providing detailed answers and recommending related products. This personalized experience increases the likelihood that the customer will complete their purchase and return in the future.

CONCLUSION: AI AS A TOOL FOR RETAINING CUSTOMERS

AI offers powerful tools for improving customer retention by predicting churn, delivering personalized re-engagement campaigns, and automating loyalty programs. By using AI to understand customer behavior, businesses can take proactive steps to address churn risks, offer personalized rewards, and create a better customer experience. This not only increases customer satisfaction but also improves long-term profitability and customer loyalty.

KEY TAKEAWAYS:

- **Churn Prediction**: AI tools like **Optimove** and **Salesforce Einstein** predict customer churn, allowing businesses to take proactive steps to retain at-risk customers.
- **Personalized Re-Engagement**: AI-powered platforms like **Klaviyo** and **ActiveCampaign** create personalized re-engagement campaigns that target customers based on their behavior and preferences.
- **Loyalty Programs**: AI-driven loyalty platforms like **LoyaltyLion** and **Smile.io** personalize rewards and incentives based on customer activity, increasing engagement and retention.
- **Sentiment Analysis**: Tools like **Zendesk** and **Medallia** use AI to track customer sentiment, helping businesses identify and resolve issues before they lead to churn.
- **Automated Retention**: AI tools automate retention campaigns, ensuring that customers receive timely and relevant offers without manual intervention.

CHAPTER 5: PRACTICAL IMPLEMENTATION AND CASE STUDIES

5.1 STEP-BY-STEP GUIDE TO AI INTEGRATION

INTRODUCTION

Artificial Intelligence (AI) is transforming the way businesses operate, offering tools to automate tasks, personalize customer experiences, optimize marketing efforts, and improve decision-making. For website owners and e-commerce businesses, integrating AI can lead to significant benefits, including increased sales, better customer retention, and more efficient operations. However, integrating AI into your website or business processes may seem daunting at first. In this lesson, we'll break down the steps to successfully integrate AI into your business, focusing on practical implementation, the tools available, and how to align AI with your business goals.

WHY INTEGRATE AI INTO YOUR WEBSITE OR BUSINESS?

AI can help businesses achieve a variety of goals, such as:

- **Improving Customer Experience**: Personalizing user interactions, offering real-time assistance through chatbots, and delivering relevant product recommendations.
- **Optimizing Operations**: Automating repetitive tasks like email marketing, customer support, and pricing adjustments, freeing up time for your team to focus on strategic tasks.
- **Enhancing Marketing Campaigns**: Using AI to optimize ad targeting, segment audiences, and create personalized content that resonates with different customer segments.
- **Data-Driven Decision Making**: Leveraging AI-powered analytics to forecast demand, predict customer behavior, and improve decision-making across various business functions.

By integrating AI, businesses can stay competitive, streamline operations, and provide a more tailored experience for customers.

DEFINE YOUR AI OBJECTIVES AND USE CASES

The first step to integrating AI is to clearly define your business objectives and identify the areas where AI can provide value. Start by assessing your current challenges and goals.

Common AI Use Cases:

- **Customer Support**: Implement AI-powered chatbots to provide instant responses and 24/7 support.
- **Personalization**: Use AI to personalize product recommendations, email content, and website experiences for each customer.
- **Marketing Automation**: Automate marketing campaigns using AI to send targeted emails, optimize ads, and segment your audience.
- **Sales Optimization**: Apply AI for dynamic pricing, predicting product demand, and upselling or cross-selling relevant products.
- **Predictive Analytics**: Use AI to analyze historical data and forecast sales, customer behavior, and market trends.

Example: If your business experiences high cart abandonment rates, you might consider using AI to automate abandoned cart emails or use AI-powered dynamic pricing to offer personalized discounts in real time.

CHOOSE THE RIGHT AI TOOLS

Once you've identified your objectives, it's time to choose the AI tools that align with your goals. There are many AI platforms available that cater to different needs, from marketing automation to customer support. The key is to find tools that integrate seamlessly with your existing systems.

Key AI Tools to Consider:

- **For Customer Support**:
  - **Tidio**: Offers AI-powered chatbots that provide instant responses and guide customers through purchasing decisions.
  - **Intercom**: Combines live chat with AI-driven automation to support customers and recommend products.
- **For Personalization**:
  - **Dynamic Yield**: Personalizes website content and product recommendations using AI to tailor experiences in real time.
  - **Nosto**: AI-driven tool that recommends personalized products based on user behavior and preferences.
- **For Marketing Automation**:
  - **Klaviyo**: AI-powered email marketing tool that segments audiences and sends personalized messages based on customer

behavior.
- **ActiveCampaign**: Uses AI to automate email workflows, segment audiences, and deliver personalized campaigns.

- **For Sales Optimization**:
  - **Prisync**: AI-powered dynamic pricing tool that adjusts prices based on market trends and competitor activity.
  - **Competera**: Provides AI-driven pricing recommendations to maximize profitability and optimize sales.

- **For Predictive Analytics**:
  - **Optimove**: AI tool that predicts customer behavior, segments audiences, and provides insights to improve customer retention.
  - **Custora**: Uses AI to analyze customer data and forecast future behaviors, helping businesses optimize their customer engagement strategies.

Example: If you want to improve your email marketing efforts, you might integrate a tool like Klaviyo, which uses AI to automatically send personalized emails based on customer behavior, boosting engagement and conversions.

COLLECT AND ORGANIZE YOUR DATA

AI relies heavily on data to function effectively. Before you can integrate AI into your business, you need to ensure that your data is organized, clean, and accessible. This step involves gathering customer data, sales data, website analytics, and other relevant information that AI will use to generate insights or automate processes.

Types of Data to Collect:

- **Customer Behavior Data**: Purchase history, browsing patterns, cart activity, and customer engagement.
- **Sales Data**: Historical sales records, product performance, and sales trends.
- **Marketing Data**: Email open rates, click-through rates, conversion data, and ad performance.
- **Customer Support Data**: Chat and support ticket history, frequently asked questions, and customer feedback.

Data Management Tips:

- Use a **Customer Relationship Management (CRM)** system, such as Salesforce or HubSpot, to store and manage customer data.
- Ensure your data is clean and accurate by regularly

reviewing and removing outdated or incorrect information.
- Make sure your data is structured and accessible, so AI tools can easily analyze it to generate actionable insights.

Example: If you plan to use AI for personalized product recommendations, make sure you have accurate customer behavior data (e.g., purchase history and browsing patterns) stored in your CRM or e-commerce platform.

INTEGRATE AI WITH YOUR EXISTING SYSTEMS

Once you've chosen your AI tools and organized your data, the next step is to integrate AI into your existing systems. Many AI platforms offer plug-and-play integrations with popular e-commerce, CRM, and marketing platforms. However, you may need to work with developers if custom integrations are required.

Common Integration Points:

- **E-commerce Platform**: Ensure your AI tools integrate with your e-commerce platform (e.g., Shopify, WooCommerce) to personalize product recommendations, optimize pricing, or track customer behavior.
- **CRM System**: Integrate AI with your CRM system (e.g., Salesforce, HubSpot) to enhance customer segmentation, forecast sales, and automate marketing efforts.
- **Marketing Platforms**: Connect AI tools to your email marketing or advertising platforms (e.g., Mailchimp, Google Ads) to automate campaigns, optimize ad targeting, and personalize content.

Steps for Integration:

1. **API Integration**: Use API connections to integrate AI tools with your website, e-commerce platform, or

CRM. Most AI platforms provide documentation to guide you through this process.

2. **Third-Party Integrations**: Leverage existing integrations, such as Shopify's App Store or Salesforce's AppExchange, to quickly connect AI tools to your systems.

3. **Custom Integration**: For more complex implementations, you may need to work with a developer to customize how AI tools integrate with your current setup.

Example: You might integrate Nosto (for personalized product recommendations) with your Shopify store, allowing the AI tool to analyze customer behavior and automatically suggest relevant products.

TEST AND MONITOR PERFORMANCE

After integrating AI, it's essential to test its functionality to ensure everything is working as expected. This step involves monitoring how well the AI is performing, reviewing the results, and making necessary adjustments to optimize the integration.

Key Metrics to Monitor:

- **Customer Engagement**: Track changes in customer engagement levels, such as click-through rates, time spent on the website, and conversion rates after AI implementation.
- **Sales and Revenue**: Monitor how AI-driven pricing, recommendations, and marketing efforts impact sales, average order value, and revenue.
- **Customer Satisfaction**: Use feedback surveys, sentiment analysis, and support data to assess how AI-driven customer support or personalization efforts are affecting customer satisfaction.
- **AI Accuracy**: Regularly review the accuracy of AI recommendations, dynamic pricing adjustments, or predictive analytics to ensure they align with your business goals.

Testing Tips:

- Start with a small test group or a specific product category before rolling out AI across your entire website or customer base.

- Run A/B tests to compare the performance of AI-driven strategies against non-AI methods to evaluate their effectiveness.
- Continuously analyze the data provided by AI tools to refine your strategies and improve performance.

Example: If you've integrated Prisync for dynamic pricing, monitor how pricing changes affect sales and revenue. Use A/B testing to compare dynamic pricing to fixed pricing and adjust based on the results.

OPTIMIZE AND SCALE YOUR AI USE

Once you've tested your AI integration and gathered insights, it's time to optimize and scale its use across your business. This may involve expanding AI tools to new areas, fine-tuning algorithms based on performance data, or adding new AI features to further enhance your operations.

Optimization Strategies:

- **Refine AI Algorithms**: Work with your AI provider to tweak algorithms based on your business's performance data and specific needs.
- **Expand AI to Other Areas**: If you started with AI for customer support, consider expanding to other areas like dynamic pricing, inventory management, or marketing automation.
- **Continuously Monitor**: Regularly review the performance of AI tools and make adjustments as needed to ensure that they continue to meet your business goals.
- **Add AI Tools**: As your business grows, you may want to introduce additional AI tools to further automate tasks, such as AI-powered inventory management or sales forecasting.

Example: After successfully using AI-powered chatbots for customer support, you might decide to integrate AI into your marketing campaigns by using Klaviyo to automate personalized email flows and re-engagement campaigns.

CONCLUSION: SUCCESSFULLY INTEGRATING AI INTO YOUR BUSINESS

Integrating AI into your website or business can significantly improve customer experience, automate tasks, and boost sales. By following the steps outlined in this lesson—defining your objectives, choosing the right tools, organizing data, integrating AI, testing, and optimizing—you can successfully incorporate AI into your business and maximize its benefits. Whether you're looking to personalize customer interactions, improve marketing efforts, or optimize pricing, AI offers the tools to drive growth and improve operational efficiency.

Key Takeaways:

- **Define Your Goals**: Identify the specific areas of your business where AI can add value, such as customer support, marketing automation, or sales optimization.
- **Choose the Right Tools**: Select AI tools that align

with your business needs, whether for customer support (e.g., **Tidio**), marketing automation (e.g., **Klaviyo**), or dynamic pricing (e.g., **Prisync**).

- **Organize Your Data**: Ensure that customer, sales, and marketing data is clean, structured, and accessible for AI analysis.
- **Test and Monitor Performance**: Regularly track AI performance metrics to ensure that your integration is meeting its objectives, and make adjustments as needed.
- **Scale and Optimize**: Continuously optimize your AI tools and explore new use cases to expand the impact of AI on your business.

5.2 REAL-WORLD CASE STUDIES OF AI INTEGRATION

INTRODUCTION

Integrating Artificial Intelligence (AI) into your business can revolutionize how you operate, but seeing how it works in real-world applications is often the key to understanding its full potential. In this lesson, we will explore real-world case studies of businesses that have successfully integrated AI into their operations. These examples will illustrate how AI tools can enhance customer service, boost sales, optimize pricing, and improve customer retention. By examining these case studies, you'll gain insights into how AI can be applied to your own business.

CASE STUDY 1: NETFLIX – PERSONALIZATION WITH AI

Overview

Netflix is one of the most well-known examples of a company using AI to drive customer satisfaction and engagement. Netflix leverages AI algorithms to personalize the content recommendations for each of its over 200 million subscribers, enhancing the user experience and increasing retention.

AI Integration

Netflix's recommendation engine analyzes a user's viewing history, search patterns, and viewing time to suggest movies and shows tailored to their preferences. The AI algorithms also take into account global trends, content similarities, and other users' behavior to continuously refine recommendations.

Results
- **Increased Engagement**: Netflix reports that 80% of the content users watch comes from personalized recommendations, showing how effective AI-powered recommendations are at driving user engagement.
- **Reduced Churn**: By offering personalized content, Netflix has been able to improve customer retention rates. Personalized recommendations keep users engaged, reducing the likelihood they will cancel their subscription.

Key Takeaway

Personalization is a powerful tool for customer retention and engagement. By using AI to deliver tailored content or product recommendations, businesses can increase user satisfaction and loyalty.

CASE STUDY 2: SEPHORA – AI-POWERED VIRTUAL ASSISTANT

Overview

Sephora, a global beauty retailer, has implemented AI to enhance customer support and improve the online shopping experience. Through AI-powered chatbots and virtual assistants, Sephora provides personalized product recommendations, beauty tips, and real-time support to its customers.

AI Integration

Sephora's AI virtual assistant, **Sephora Virtual Artist**, uses machine learning to recommend products based on a customer's skin tone, facial features, and preferences. The assistant helps customers visualize how makeup products will look on their faces using augmented reality (AR). Additionally, Sephora's chatbots assist customers with product searches, answer questions, and provide personalized beauty advice.

Results

- **Improved Customer Experience**: Sephora's virtual assistant significantly improved the customer experience by offering instant, personalized product recommendations, reducing friction in the purchasing process.
- **Increased Sales**: By using AI-powered personalization and providing virtual try-ons, Sephora saw a significant increase in conversion rates and average order value.
- **Higher Customer Satisfaction**: Sephora's chatbots improved response times and customer satisfaction by providing immediate assistance without needing human intervention.

Key Takeaway

AI-powered chatbots and virtual assistants can enhance the customer experience by offering instant, personalized support. This improves engagement, boosts conversion rates, and builds stronger customer relationships.

CASE STUDY 3: AMAZON – AI FOR DYNAMIC PRICING AND INVENTORY MANAGEMENT

Overview

Amazon, the world's largest online retailer, uses AI extensively for dynamic pricing, personalized recommendations, and inventory management. AI helps Amazon adjust prices in real time, predict demand, and optimize inventory across its vast global network.

AI Integration

Amazon's AI-driven dynamic pricing algorithm adjusts product prices multiple times a day based on factors such as demand, competitor prices, market trends, and inventory levels. This enables Amazon to stay competitive while optimizing profitability. Additionally, Amazon uses AI to forecast product demand, ensuring its inventory is efficiently managed and restocked as needed.

Results

- **Increased Revenue**: Dynamic pricing allows Amazon to maximize revenue by responding to real-time market conditions, increasing sales while optimizing profit margins.
- **Improved Inventory Management**: AI-driven demand forecasting has improved Amazon's ability to manage its inventory, reducing stockouts and minimizing excess inventory costs.
- **Competitive Advantage**: AI helps Amazon stay ahead of its competitors by constantly adjusting prices and inventory based on real-time data, offering customers the best possible deals.

Key Takeaway

Dynamic pricing and demand forecasting powered by AI allow businesses to maximize revenue and optimize inventory management. These tools can help maintain competitiveness, improve sales, and enhance operational efficiency.

CASE STUDY 4: STARBUCKS

AI FOR CUSTOMER RETENTION AND PERSONALIZATION

Overview

Starbucks uses AI to drive customer loyalty and retention through its mobile app, personalized offers, and recommendations. The Starbucks app, powered by AI, creates a highly personalized experience by analyzing customer behavior, purchase history, and preferences.

AI Integration

The Starbucks app uses AI to predict what customers are most likely to order based on their previous behavior. The app then sends personalized drink and food recommendations and offers, such as discounts or loyalty points, to encourage repeat purchases. Additionally, Starbucks uses AI to optimize inventory at its locations, ensuring popular items are always in stock.

Results

- **Increased Customer Retention**: Personalized offers and loyalty rewards sent through the app have contributed to higher customer retention and engagement rates. Customers are more likely to return when they feel valued and receive relevant offers.
- **Higher Average Order Value**: AI-powered recommendations have increased the average order value by suggesting complementary items and personalized promotions.
- **Enhanced Customer Experience**: The app's seamless experience, powered by AI, has improved customer satisfaction and convenience, further driving loyalty.

Key Takeaway

AI can help businesses retain customers and increase sales by delivering personalized offers, rewards, and recommendations. By making customers feel valued, businesses can drive repeat purchases and boost overall engagement.

CASE STUDY 5: H&M – AI FOR SUPPLY CHAIN OPTIMIZATION

Overview

H&M, one of the world's largest fashion retailers, uses AI to optimize its supply chain, manage inventory, and improve demand forecasting. This allows H&M to make better decisions about product replenishment, reduce waste, and increase efficiency.

AI Integration

H&M leverages AI to analyze sales data, market trends, and consumer behavior to predict which products will be in demand. AI also helps optimize the supply chain by determining the best times to restock items, which stores to allocate inventory to, and when to mark down products based on sales velocity and demand patterns.

Results

- **Reduced Inventory Costs**: By using AI to forecast demand more accurately, H&M has been able to reduce excess inventory, minimizing costs associated with overstocking.
- **Improved Product Availability**: AI-driven demand forecasting has improved H&M's ability to stock the right products at the right time, ensuring customers can find what they need.

- **More Efficient Supply Chain**: AI optimization has streamlined H&M's supply chain operations, reducing delays and improving overall efficiency.

Key Takeaway

AI can greatly improve supply chain management and inventory forecasting. Businesses that use AI to predict demand and optimize inventory can reduce costs, improve product availability, and increase operational efficiency.

CONCLUSION: REAL-WORLD AI SUCCESSES

These real-world case studies demonstrate the immense potential of AI across different industries and business models. From personalization and dynamic pricing to customer retention and supply chain optimization, AI provides actionable insights, automates complex processes, and drives significant improvements in customer satisfaction and profitability.

KEY TAKEAWAYS:

- **Netflix**: AI-driven personalization boosts engagement and reduces customer churn by offering tailored content recommendations.
- **Sephora**: AI-powered virtual assistants improve the customer shopping experience with personalized recommendations and virtual try-ons.
- **Amazon**: Dynamic pricing and demand forecasting, powered by AI, maximize sales and optimize inventory management.
- **Starbucks**: AI enhances customer retention by delivering personalized offers and loyalty rewards through its mobile app.
- **H&M**: AI improves supply chain efficiency by optimizing demand forecasting and inventory management, reducing costs, and enhancing product availability.

5.3 COMMON CHALLENGES AND SOLUTIONS

INTRODUCTION

While the benefits of Artificial Intelligence (AI) for businesses are undeniable—boosting productivity, improving customer experiences, and increasing sales—many companies face challenges in adopting AI. Common barriers include misconceptions about AI, fears about its complexity, concerns about costs, and questions about its return on investment (ROI). In this lesson, we'll tackle these challenges head-on, offering practical solutions to overcome adoption barriers, manage costs, and measure the impact of AI on your business.

OVERCOMING AI ADOPTION BARRIERS: ADDRESSING COMMON FEARS AND MISCONCEPTIONS

Adopting AI may seem overwhelming to many businesses, especially for those unfamiliar with the technology. Misconceptions and fears about AI's complexity, potential job displacement, and loss of control can slow or prevent its adoption. Let's address these concerns and offer solutions to overcome them.

COMMON FEARS AND MISCONCEPTIONS ABOUT AI:

- **Fear of Job Displacement**: One of the most common fears surrounding AI is that it will replace human jobs. Many employees worry that AI will automate tasks that were traditionally performed by people, leading to layoffs or reduced roles.
- **Complexity of AI**: AI is often perceived as highly technical, requiring expert-level knowledge in data science, machine learning, and programming. For businesses without in-house expertise, AI can seem too complicated to implement.
- **Loss of Control Over Decision-Making**: Some business leaders worry that relying on AI for decision-making will lead to a loss of control, as AI systems may make decisions based on algorithms that are difficult to fully understand.
- **Uncertainty About AI's Usefulness**: Businesses may be skeptical about whether AI can truly deliver on its promises. Many question whether AI will yield tangible improvements in efficiency, sales, or customer satisfaction.

SOLUTIONS TO OVERCOME AI ADOPTION BARRIERS

AI as a Job Enhancer, Not a Job Replacer

Instead of seeing AI as a job threat, businesses should recognize AI as a tool to **enhance employee productivity** by automating repetitive, low-level tasks. This allows employees to focus on more strategic, creative, and high-value work. AI empowers human workers rather than replacing them, enabling businesses to innovate and grow.

- **Example**: In customer service, AI chatbots can handle simple inquiries 24/7, but complex or high-value customer interactions still require human input. The AI assists in managing high volumes of routine tasks, while employees can focus on building deeper customer relationships.

START SIMPLE: USER-FRIENDLY AI SOLUTIONS

You don't need a data scientist to integrate AI into your business. Many AI platforms offer **low-code or no-code solutions**, meaning you can get started without technical expertise. Popular AI tools come with intuitive interfaces, making it easy to implement AI for customer support, marketing automation, or sales optimization.

- **Example**: AI-powered tools like **Tidio** for customer service or **Klaviyo** for email marketing provide user-friendly dashboards, enabling businesses to automate customer interactions and marketing campaigns without requiring deep AI expertise.

HYBRID DECISION-MAKING: COMBINING AI WITH HUMAN JUDGMENT

AI should be viewed as a tool to **enhance decision-making**, not replace it. Business leaders can combine AI's data-driven insights with human intuition and experience to make informed decisions. AI can help analyze vast datasets and surface trends, but human oversight remains crucial to interpreting those insights and aligning them with broader business goals.

- **Example**: AI can recommend pricing strategies based on real-time data, but human managers can adjust those recommendations based on external factors, such as upcoming product launches or market shifts.

BEGIN WITH HIGH-IMPACT, LOW-RISK AI USE CASES

Businesses that are uncertain about the potential of AI should start with **small, high-impact use cases** where the benefits are easy to measure. For example, automating email marketing, using chatbots for basic customer queries, or deploying AI for product recommendations are practical applications that can deliver clear, measurable improvements.

- **Example**: A small e-commerce business might start by integrating an AI-powered email automation tool like **Mailchimp**, which segments customers and sends personalized emails based on past purchases, leading to improved open rates and conversions.

MANAGING COSTS AND ROI: HOW TO IMPLEMENT AI AFFORDABLY AND MEASURE THE RETURN ON INVESTMENT

Many businesses worry that implementing AI is prohibitively expensive and fear they won't see a sufficient return on their investment. While it's true that some AI solutions can be costly, there are ways to manage costs and measure ROI effectively.

HOW TO IMPLEMENT AI AFFORDABLY

Start Small and Scale Gradually

One of the most cost-effective ways to integrate AI is by starting with **small, affordable AI tools** that address specific business needs, then scaling gradually as you see success. You don't need to overhaul your entire business with AI all at once.

- **Example**: A small retailer might use a low-cost AI chatbot like **ManyChat** to handle simple customer service tasks. As the business grows and the chatbot proves successful, they can invest in more advanced AI tools for inventory management or marketing automation.

LEVERAGE CLOUD-BASED AI SERVICES

Cloud-based AI services, such as **Google Cloud AI** or **AWS AI**, offer pay-as-you-go pricing models, allowing businesses to scale their AI usage according to their needs. This eliminates the need for significant upfront infrastructure costs and reduces the financial risk of AI implementation.

- **Example**: By using **Google Cloud AI's** machine learning tools, businesses can only pay for the resources they use, making AI more accessible and affordable for small and medium-sized businesses.

CHOOSE AI TOOLS WITH FLEXIBLE PRICING PLANS

Many AI platforms offer **tiered pricing plans** that cater to businesses of different sizes. Start with basic or entry-level plans, then upgrade as your business grows and your AI needs expand. Many platforms also offer free trials, allowing businesses to test AI capabilities before committing to a subscription.

- **Example**: **Klaviyo**, an AI-powered marketing tool, offers flexible pricing based on the number of contacts you have, making it easy for small businesses to start with a low-cost plan and scale as their email list grows.

AUTOMATE REPETITIVE TASKS TO MAXIMIZE ROI

AI's true value lies in its ability to automate repetitive tasks, such as customer support, email marketing, or inventory management. Automating these processes saves time and reduces labor costs, delivering a clear and measurable ROI.

- **Example**: By implementing AI-powered inventory management tools like **Inventory Planner**, businesses can optimize stock levels, reduce overstock costs, and improve sales forecasting—all of which contribute to increased profitability.

HOW TO MEASURE AI'S RETURN ON INVESTMENT (ROI)

Measuring AI's ROI involves analyzing how AI impacts your business's bottom line by improving efficiency, increasing sales, or enhancing customer satisfaction. Here's how to measure AI's ROI effectively:

DEFINE CLEAR GOALS AND METRICS

Before integrating AI, set **clear goals** for what you hope to achieve, such as increasing sales, improving customer retention, or reducing operational costs. Define specific **metrics** that will help you measure the success of your AI initiative, such as conversion rates, customer lifetime value (CLV), or response times.

- **Example**: If your goal is to increase customer retention, measure how AI-powered personalized offers or loyalty programs impact your customer churn rate.

CALCULATE COST SAVINGS FROM AUTOMATION

AI-driven automation often leads to reduced labor costs and increased operational efficiency. Calculate the cost savings from automating tasks that would otherwise require manual intervention, such as responding to customer queries, sending marketing emails, or adjusting pricing.

- **Example**: A business using an AI-powered customer service chatbot like **Tidio** might see a reduction in customer support staff workload, leading to savings on labor costs and faster response times for customers.

TRACK REVENUE GROWTH AND CONVERSION RATES

AI tools that improve sales and marketing, such as product recommendation engines or personalized email campaigns, can drive revenue growth by increasing conversion rates and boosting average order values. Monitor changes in key sales metrics before and after AI implementation to assess ROI.

- **Example**: By implementing **Nosto** for AI-powered product recommendations, a business can track how these personalized suggestions increase the average order value and contribute to overall revenue growth.

ANALYZE LONG-TERM CUSTOMER RETENTION AND SATISFACTION

AI can improve customer experiences through personalization, leading to higher satisfaction and long-term loyalty. Use customer retention metrics, satisfaction scores, and reviews to gauge how AI impacts customer relationships over time.

- **Example**: Starbucks uses AI in its loyalty app to offer personalized drink recommendations and rewards, contributing to higher customer retention and satisfaction scores. Businesses can track customer lifetime value (CLV) to measure long-term returns from these AI-driven strategies.

CONCLUSION: OVERCOMING AI ADOPTION BARRIERS AND MEASURING ROI

Integrating AI into your business is a powerful way to automate processes, improve customer experiences, and drive growth. However, overcoming common fears and misconceptions, managing costs, and measuring the impact of AI are crucial to a successful AI strategy. By starting small, focusing on high-impact use cases, and using affordable, scalable tools, businesses can realize the benefits of AI without overwhelming costs. Additionally, by setting clear goals and tracking performance, businesses can accurately measure AI's ROI, ensuring long-term success.

KEY TAKEAWAYS:

- **Overcoming AI Fears**: AI is not here to replace jobs but to enhance productivity. Start with simple AI tools that require minimal technical expertise and view AI as a tool to enhance human decision-making, not replace it.

- **Managing Costs**: Start small, use affordable cloud-based AI services, and automate repetitive tasks to drive cost savings. Use tools with flexible pricing plans that align with your business's growth.

- **Measuring ROI**: Define clear goals and metrics for AI implementation, track cost savings from automation, monitor revenue growth and conversion rates, and analyze long-term customer retention and satisfaction to measure the success of AI initiatives.

CHAPTER 6:
FINAL PROJECT

6.1 Setting Up Your AI Strategy

INTRODUCTION

Setting up an AI strategy for your website is key to unlocking the full potential of Artificial Intelligence. With a clear plan in place, you can use AI tools to achieve specific business goals such as increasing traffic, improving conversions, and enhancing customer retention. In this lesson, we'll walk you through the steps to create an effective AI strategy. This will involve defining your goals, selecting the right AI tools, and developing a 3-month action plan to integrate AI into your website and business operations.

DEFINE YOUR GOALS: WHAT DO YOU WANT TO ACHIEVE WITH AI?

The foundation of a successful AI strategy is setting clear, measurable goals. These goals will shape how you choose AI tools and how you integrate them into your business.

COMMON AI-DRIVEN GOALS:

- **Increased Website Traffic**: Use AI to optimize your content for search engines, personalize marketing efforts, and target the right audiences to drive more visitors to your site.
- **Higher Conversion Rates**: Implement AI-driven personalization and dynamic pricing to encourage visitors to take action, whether it's making a purchase, signing up for a service, or completing a form.
- **Better Customer Retention**: Use AI tools to engage customers with personalized offers, automate follow-ups, and build long-term loyalty.
- **Operational Efficiency**: Automate routine tasks, such as customer support, inventory management, or marketing campaigns, to save time and resources.

Example Goals:

- **Increase website traffic by 20% in 3 months** through AI-powered SEO optimization and targeted marketing campaigns.
- **Boost conversion rates by 15%** by using AI to deliver personalized product recommendations and dynamic pricing.
- **Improve customer retention by 25%** by using AI to automate personalized email campaigns and loyalty programs.

SELECT AND INTEGRATE AI TOOLS BASED ON YOUR OBJECTIVES

Once you've defined your goals, the next step is to select the right AI tools that align with those objectives. AI platforms offer a wide range of capabilities, from customer service automation and marketing optimization to personalized recommendations and sales forecasting. Choose tools that fit your budget, business needs, and technical capabilities.

AI TOOLS FOR COMMON OBJECTIVES:

Objective: Increase Website Traffic

- **Surfer SEO**: An AI-powered tool that helps optimize your content for search engines by analyzing keywords, competitor content, and SEO best practices.
- **HubSpot**: AI-driven CRM and marketing automation that allows you to target the right audience, drive traffic through personalized campaigns, and track lead generation efforts.

Objective: Improve Conversion Rates

- **Nosto**: Provides AI-powered personalized product recommendations and dynamic content to drive higher conversion rates.
- **Prisync**: AI-powered dynamic pricing tool that adjusts product prices in real time based on market trends and competitor activity, encouraging more purchases.

Objective: Enhance Customer Retention

- **Klaviyo**: AI-driven email marketing platform that automates personalized email campaigns based on customer behavior, purchase history, and engagement.
- **LoyaltyLion**: An AI-powered loyalty platform that

personalizes rewards and loyalty programs based on customer activity, driving repeat purchases and engagement.

Objective: Increase Operational Efficiency

- **Tidio**: AI-powered chatbot that automates customer service, answering common questions and freeing up your support team for more complex tasks.
- **ActiveCampaign**: AI-driven marketing automation tool that segments your audience, automates campaigns, and optimizes your marketing strategy to save time.

CREATE A 3-MONTH AI ACTION PLAN

To ensure your AI integration is successful, create a clear, step-by-step action plan. Your plan should outline how you will implement AI tools, monitor progress, and adjust strategies over the next three months. By focusing on short-term milestones, you can track progress and make data-driven decisions to optimize your AI efforts.

STEP 1: MONTH 1 - SET UP AND INITIAL INTEGRATION

In the first month, focus on setting up and integrating your chosen AI tools. This phase involves connecting AI platforms to your website, configuring them to meet your business needs, and testing their functionality.

Key Actions:

1. **Select AI Tools**: Choose the AI tools that align with your business goals (e.g., Nosto for product recommendations, Klaviyo for email automation).
2. **Integration**: Integrate the tools with your website, e-commerce platform, or CRM. This may involve connecting APIs, setting up plugins, or working with developers for custom integrations.
3. **Data Collection**: Ensure that your AI tools have access to the data they need (e.g., customer behavior, sales data, marketing analytics) to function effectively.
4. **Run Initial Tests**: Test each AI tool to ensure it's working as expected, such as verifying that product recommendations are relevant or that automated emails are sent correctly.

Example: During Month 1, integrate Klaviyo with your Shopify store and start segmenting your email list based on customer purchase history. Set up basic email automation flows, such as abandoned cart reminders or

welcome emails for new subscribers.

STEP 2: MONTH 2 - MONITOR PERFORMANCE AND OPTIMIZE

In Month 2, focus on monitoring the performance of your AI tools and making necessary adjustments. At this stage, you should gather data on how well the tools are performing and use it to refine your AI-driven processes.

Key Actions:

1. **Monitor Key Metrics**: Track important KPIs related to your goals, such as conversion rates, traffic growth, email open rates, and customer engagement.
2. **A/B Testing**: Use A/B testing to compare the performance of AI-driven strategies against traditional methods (e.g., AI-powered product recommendations vs. manual recommendations).
3. **Optimize Based on Data**: Make adjustments to your AI tools based on the data collected. For example, refine your email campaigns based on open and click-through rates or adjust pricing strategies based on sales data.
4. **Engage Customers**: Start launching AI-powered campaigns, such as personalized email flows or product recommendations, and track how customers

respond.

Example: In Month 2, analyze how Nosto is influencing conversions on your website. Use A/B testing to compare the conversion rates of visitors who receive personalized recommendations against those who don't. Optimize the recommendation engine based on product performance data.

STEP 3: MONTH 3 - SCALE AND EXPAND AI USE

By the third month, you should have a clear understanding of which AI strategies are working best for your business. Now, you can scale your AI efforts, expand to new areas, and fine-tune your strategy for long-term success.

Key Actions:

1. **Scale AI Campaigns**: Expand successful AI-driven campaigns, such as increasing the number of personalized emails you send or introducing dynamic pricing to more product categories.
2. **Introduce New AI Tools**: If your initial AI integrations have been successful, consider introducing additional AI tools that complement your business goals, such as AI for inventory management or customer segmentation.
3. **Analyze Overall Impact**: Review the results of your AI strategy over the past three months. Evaluate its impact on your key business metrics, such as traffic, conversions, customer retention, and efficiency.
4. **Set Long-Term AI Goals**: Based on your results, set new, long-term AI goals for the next six months to a year. Identify areas where AI can deliver even more value and plan how you'll further integrate AI into your business.

Example: In Month 3, if Klaviyo has successfully increased customer engagement through personalized email flows, expand those campaigns to new customer segments (e.g., VIP customers, inactive customers). Set up additional automation workflows to scale your email marketing efforts.

CONCLUSION: BUILDING A SUCCESSFUL AI STRATEGY

Setting up an AI strategy involves defining your business goals, selecting the right AI tools, and creating a clear action plan to implement and optimize AI over time. By taking a structured approach, you can ensure that AI delivers tangible results, from increasing website traffic and conversions to improving customer retention and operational efficiency.

KEY TAKEAWAYS

- **Define Clear AI Goals**: Identify specific objectives like increasing traffic, improving conversion rates, or enhancing customer retention to guide your AI strategy.
- **Select the Right Tools**: Choose AI tools that align with your goals, such as **Nosto** for personalized recommendations, **Klaviyo** for email automation, or **Surfer SEO** for content optimization.
- **Create a 3-Month Action Plan**: Implement your AI tools over three months by focusing on integration, monitoring, optimization, and scaling successful AI campaigns.

CONCLUSION: HARNESSING AI FOR BUSINESS GROWTH

This book has taken you on a journey through the transformative power of Artificial Intelligence (AI) and how it can revolutionize your website, operations, and customer interactions. By now, you should have a deep understanding of how AI can be integrated into various aspects of your business, from marketing and sales to customer support and data-driven decision-making.

KEY TAKEAWAYS FROM THIS BOOK

1. **AI as a Growth Driver**: AI is no longer just a tool for large corporations—it's accessible to businesses of all sizes. Whether you're an e-commerce store, a service provider, or a content creator, AI can help you increase traffic, improve conversions, and optimize operations.

2. **Personalization is Key**: One of AI's greatest strengths lies in its ability to deliver personalized experiences at scale. By tailoring content, product recommendations, and marketing messages to individual users, you can significantly boost customer engagement and loyalty.

3. **Automation Unlocks Efficiency**: AI allows businesses to automate repetitive tasks such as customer service, email marketing, and data analysis, freeing up valuable time for strategic initiatives. This automation not only reduces operational costs but also ensures that your business can operate around the clock.

4. **Data-Driven Decision Making**: AI helps you turn data into actionable insights. From predicting customer behavior to optimizing pricing strategies, AI empowers you to make informed decisions that

drive growth and profitability.
5. **Overcoming AI Challenges**: The integration of AI comes with challenges, including data quality, cost concerns, and managing customer expectations. However, with careful planning, strategic tool selection, and continuous optimization, these challenges can be overcome.

THE FUTURE OF AI IN BUSINESS

AI's capabilities are growing rapidly, and its role in business will continue to expand. As machine learning models become more sophisticated, and as AI tools become more user-friendly and accessible, businesses will have even more opportunities to leverage AI for competitive advantage. By staying informed about AI trends and continuously exploring new ways to integrate AI into your operations, you can stay ahead of the curve and ensure sustained business growth.

YOUR NEXT STEPS

- **Refine Your AI Strategy**: Revisit your AI goals and ensure that they align with your long-term business objectives. Whether it's expanding into predictive analytics, enhancing customer retention, or streamlining operations, AI should be at the heart of your growth strategy.
- **Scale AI Gradually**: Start by implementing AI in key areas of your business, and once you see positive results, scale it to other areas like inventory management, marketing optimization, and customer service.
- **Stay Curious**: AI is evolving quickly, so continue learning about the latest advancements and tools in the AI space. Experiment with new AI technologies as they emerge and adapt them to your business model.

FINAL THOUGHT

AI has the potential to reshape the future of business. By integrating AI into your operations, you're not only enhancing your current performance but also preparing your business for a future where intelligent systems will play an even greater role. The opportunities AI offers are vast—embrace them, experiment, and watch your business grow in ways you may not have thought possible.

Thank you for exploring the world of AI through this book, and here's to your continued success as you harness the power of AI to transform your business!

www.ingramcontent.com/pod-product-compliance
Lightning Source LLC
Chambersburg PA
CBHW052140220526
45471CB00004B/1450